OUT-OF-THE-BOX BRAINTEASERS

Paul Sloane & Des MacHale

STERLING INNOVATION
An imprint of Sterling Publishing Co., Inc.

New York / London

STERLING, the Sterling logo, STERLING INNOVATION,
and the Sterling Innovation logo
are registered trademarks of Sterling Publishing Co., Inc.

2 4 6 8 10 9 7 5 3

Published by Sterling Publishing Co., Inc.
387 Park Avenue South, New York, NY 10016
© 2009 by Sterling Publishing Co., Inc.

This book is comprised of material from the following Sterling titles:
Super Lateral Thinking Puzzles © 2000 by Sloane & MacHale
Outstanding Lateral Thinking Puzzles © 2005 by Sloane & MacHale
All images used under license from Shutterstock.com

Distributed in Canada by Sterling Publishing
℅ Canadian Manda Group, 165 Dufferin Street
Toronto, Ontario, Canada M6K 3H6
Distributed in the United Kingdom by GMC Distribution Services
Castle Place, 166 High Street, Lewes, East Sussex, England BN7 1XU
Distributed in Australia by Capricorn Link (Australia) Pty. Ltd.
P.O. Box 704, Windsor, NSW 2756, Australia

Printed in China
All rights reserved

Sterling ISBN 978-1-4027-6761-6

For information about custom editions, special sales, premium and
corporate purchases, please contact Sterling Special Sales
Department at 800-805-5489 or specialsales@sterlingpublishing.com.

Acknowledgments

We would like to acknowledge the contribution of puzzle fans from all around the world (including many visitors to www.lateralpuzzles.com) who have encouraged and helped us. In particular we would like to thank Peter Bloxsom for "Down Periscope," Micheal O'Fiachra for "Shoe Shop Shuffle," Jason Burge for "Quarters," João Gonçalves for "Oskar," Torgeir Apeland for "A Difference in Attitude," Kate Fallon for "Bump," Micheal O'Fiachra for "Racing Certainty," Andrew Katz for "Cheaper by the Dozen," Brian Hobbs for "Death by Reading," Lynne Payne for "Elementary," David Burn for "Deadly Talk" and "Second of One," and Felicia Ackerman for "The Fruit of Sarcasm." Ann Sloane, Hannah Sloane, and Natasha Rawdon-Jones helped edit the book and vet the clues.

Contents

Introduction

A man was held in a high-security prison and closely watched. His wife sent him a letter in which she asked, "Should I plant the potatoes in the garden now?" He replied, "Do not plant anything in the garden. That is where I hid the guns." A little later he received another letter from his wife saying, "Many policemen came to our house. They dug up the whole garden but they did not find anything." He wrote back, "Now is the time to plant the potatoes."

That man used a little lateral thinking to solve his wife's gardening problem—and so can we all. We need new and creative ways of problem-solving, and more and more people see lateral thinking puzzles as a way to fire up this process. Trainers use these puzzles in management training courses to force managers to check their assumptions; teachers use them in class to stimulate and reward children; parents use them on long journeys to amuse and challenge the family. In all cases, the procedure is similar. One person knows the answer and he or she answers questions from the other players. The questions can be answered with "Yes," "No," or "Irrelevant."

So check all of your assumptions, ask good questions, use your imagination, think differently, and have fun solving these puzzles!

—Paul Sloane & Des MacHale

THE PUZZLES

The Deadly Sculpture

A penniless sculptor made a beautiful metal statue, which he sold. Because of this he died soon afterward. Why?

Clues: 90; Answer: 134

Peak Performance

The body of a climber is found many years after his death a thousand feet below the summit of one of the world's highest mountains. In his pocket is a diary claiming that he had reached the summit and was on his way down. How was it discovered that he was not telling the truth?

Clues: 90; Answer: 134

The Fatal Fish

A man was preparing a fish to eat for a meal when he made a mistake. He then knew that he would shortly die. How?

Clues: 90; Answer: 134

Adam Had None

Adam had none. Eve had two. Everyone nowadays has three. What are they?

Clues: 90; Answer: 134

Shot Dead

A woman who was in a house saw a stranger walking down the road. She took a gun and shot him dead. The next day she did the same thing to another stranger. Other people saw her do it and knew that she had killed the two men, yet she was never arrested or charged. Why not?

Clues: 91; Answer: 135

Would You Believe It?

Three people were holding identical blocks of wood. They released the blocks at the same time. The blocks of wood were not attached to anything. The first person's block fell downward. The second person's block rose up. The third person's block stayed where it was, unsupported. What was going on?

Clues: 91; Answer: 135

Jailbreak

A man planned his escape from prison very carefully. He could have carried it out in the dead of night but he preferred to do it in the middle of the morning. Why?

Clues: 91; Answer: 135

Sitting Ducks

Why does a woman with no interest in hunting buy a gun for shooting ducks?

Clues: 91; Answer: 136

Bald Facts

Mary, Queen of Scots was almost totally bald, and wore a wig to conceal this fact from her subjects. How was her secret revealed?

Clues: 92; Answer: 136

Lethal Action

Brazilian authorities took actions to protect their fruit crops, and ten people from another continent died. How?

Clues: 92; Answer: 136

Recognition

John lived in England all his life, until his parents died. He then went to Australia to visit relatives. His Aunt Mary had left England before he was born and had never returned. He had never met his Aunt Mary, had never spoken to her, and had never seen a picture of her. Yet he recognized her immediately in a crowded airport. How?

Clues: 92; Answer: 136

Destruction

Commercial premises are destroyed by a customer. Afterward he disappears, but even if he had been caught he could not have been charged. Why?

Clues: 92; Answer: 137

Pesky Escalator

A foreign visitor to London wanted to ride up the escalator at the subway station, but did not do so. Why?

Clues: 93; Answer: 137

Wonderful Walk

A man and his dog went for a walk in the woods. When he returned home he invented something now worth millions of dollars. What was it?

Clues: 93; Answer: 137

Poles Apart

How did early explorers economize with provisions for a polar expedition?

Clues: 93; Answer: 137

Arrested Development

A bank robber grabbed several thousand dollars from a bank counter and, although he was armed, he was captured within a few seconds before he could leave the bank. How?

Clues: 93; Answer: 138

Holed Out

A golfer dreamed all his life of getting a hole in one. However, when he eventually did get a hole in one, he was very unhappy and, in fact, quit golf altogether. Why?

Clues: 93; Answer: 138

Trunk-ated

The police stop a car and they suspect that the trunk contains evidence linking the driver with a serious crime. However, they do not have a search warrant and if they open the trunk forcibly without probable cause, any evidence uncovered will not be admissible in court. How do they proceed?

Clues: 94; Answer: 138

Sports Mad

Why was a keen sports fan rushing around his house looking for a roll of sticky tape?

Clues: 94; Answer: 139

Appendectomy I & II

(There are two different solutions to this puzzle. Try both before looking at the answer to either.)

Why did a surgeon remove a perfectly healthy appendix?

Clues: 94; Answers: 139

Riotous Assembly

After riots in a large institution, one section did not reopen for a long time after the other sections. Why?

Clues: 94; Answer: 139

Kneed to Know

A woman places her hand on her husband's knee for an hour and then takes it off for ten minutes; then she places her hand on her husband's knee for another hour. Why?

Clues: 95; Answer: 139

Bad Trip

An anti-drug agency distributed material to children in school. However, this had the opposite effect to what was intended. Why?

Clues: 95; Answer: 140

Wally Test I

From the World Association of Learning, Laughter, and Youth (WALLY) comes the WALLY Test! It is a set of quick-fire questions. They may look easy, but be warned—they are designed to trick you. Write down your answers on a piece of paper and then see how many you got right. The time limit is three minutes.

1. When you see geese flying in a V formation, why is it that one leg of the V is always longer than the other?
2. Why are there so many Smiths in the telephone directory?
3. What is E.T. short for?
4. Where do you find a no-legged dog?
5. Approximately how many house bricks does it take to complete a brick house in England?
6. How do you stop a bull from charging?
7. What cheese is made backward?
8. Take away my first letter; I remain the same. Now take away my fourth letter; I remain the same. Now take away my last letter; I remain the same. What am I?
9. If a white man threw a black stone into the Red Sea, what would it become?
10. How do you make a bandstand?

Answers: 190

Two Letters

Why did a man write the same two letters over and over again on a piece of paper?

Clues: 95; Answer: 140

Body of Evidence

A woman goes into a police station and destroys vital evidence relating to a serious crime, yet she walks away scot-free. How come?

Clues: 95; Answer: 140

Shakespeare's Blunder

What major scientific blunder did Shakespeare include in his play Twelfth Night?

Clues: 96; Answer: 140

No Charge

A man guilty of a serious crime was arrested. The police had clear evidence against him, but he was set free without charge. Why?

Clues: 96; Answer: 140

Pond Life

Why did the fashion for silk hats in the U.S. lead to a positive environmental increase in the number of small lakes and bogs?

Clues: 96; Answer: 141

Shoe Shop Shuffle

In a small town there are four shoe shops of about the same size, each carrying more or less the same line in shoes. Yet one shop loses three times as many shoes to theft as each of the other shops. Why?

Clues: 96; Answer: 141

Caesar's Blunder

Julius Caesar unexpectedly lost many of his ships when he invaded Britain. Why?

Clues: 97; Answer: 141

Slow Death

The ancient Greek playwright Aeschylus was killed by a tortoise. How?

Clues: 97; Answer: 141

Driving Away

A man steals a very expensive car owned by a very rich woman. Although he was a very good driver, within a few minutes he was involved in a serious accident. Why?

Clues: 97; Answer: 142

Lit Too Well?

Local government authorities in Sussex, England, installed many more lights than were needed. This resulted in considerable damage, but the authorities were pleased with the results. Why?

Clues: 98; Answer: 142

Quick on the Draw

Every Saturday night, the national lottery is drawn with a multimillion-dollar first prize. A man sat down in front of his TV on Saturday night and saw that the numbers drawn exactly matched the numbers on his ticket for that day's lottery. He was thrilled but did not win a penny. Why not?

Clues: 98; Answer: 142

Scaled Down

A butcher tried to deceive a customer by pressing down on the scale while weighing a turkey to make it appear heavier than it was. But the customer's subsequent order forced the butcher to admit his deception. How?

Clues: 98; Answer: 142

The Happy Woman

A woman going on a journey used a driver. Then she stopped and used a club to hit a large bird. She was very pleased. Why?

Clues: 98; Answer: 143

Vandal Scandal

The authorities in Athens were very concerned that tourists sometimes hacked pieces of marble from the columns of the ancient Parthenon buildings. The practice was illegal, but some people seemed determined to take away souvenirs. How did the authorities stop this vandalism?

Clues: 99; Answer: 143

The Deadly Drawing

A woman walked into a room and saw a new picture there. She immediately knew that someone had been killed. How?

Clues: 99; Answer: 143

Leonardo's Secret

Leonardo da Vinci created some secret designs for his paintings that he did not want anyone to see. He hid them, but they were recently discovered. How?

Clues: 99; Answer: 144

Down Periscope

A normal submarine was on the surface of the sea with its hatches open. It sailed due east for two miles. Then it stopped and went down 30 feet. It then sailed another half mile before going down a further 30 feet. All this time it kept its hatches fully open. The crew survived and were not alarmed in any way. What was going on?

Clues: 99; Answer: 144

The Letter Left Out

For mathematical reasons, in codes and ciphers it is desirable to have 25 (which is a perfect square) letters rather than the usual 26. Which letter of the English alphabet is left out and why?

Clues: 100; Answer: 144

Arrested Development—Again

Two masked men robbed a bank, but they were very quickly picked up by the police. Why?

Clues: 100; Answer: 144

Titanic Proportions

How did the sinking of the Titanic lead directly to the sinking of another ship?

Clues: 100; Answer: 144

The Mover

What can go from there to here by disappearing and then go from here to there by appearing?

Clues: 100; Answer: 144

Death of a Player

A sportsman was rushed to a hospital from where he was playing and died shortly afterward. Why?

Clues: 101; Answer: 145

Hot Picture

A woman paid an artist a large sum to create a picture, and she was very pleased with the results. Yet within a week, under her instructions, the picture was burned. Why?

Clues: 101; Answer: 145

Genuine Article

A new play by Shakespeare is discovered. How did the literary experts prove it was authentic?

Clues: 101; Answer: 145

Unhealthy Lifestyle

A man and a woman were exploring in the jungle. The woman had a very healthy lifestyle, while the man had a very unhealthy one. At the end of the exploration the woman died suddenly, but the man lived. Why?

Clues: 102; Answer: 146

New World Record

A 102-year-old woman was infirm and inactive, yet one day she was congratulated on setting a new world record. What was it?

Clues: 102; Answer: 146

Death by Romance

A newly married couple had a fireside supper together. They were so cozy and comfortable that they dozed off on the floor. Next morning they were both found dead where they lay. What had happened?

Clues: 102; Answer: 146

Penalty

After a World Cup soccer match, two players swapped jerseys. The police immediately arrested them. Why?

Clues: 102; Answer: 147

Golf Challenge I, II, & III

(There are three different solutions to this puzzle. Try all three before looking at any of the answers.) A man and a woman, who were both poor golfers, challenged each other to a match. The man scored 96 while the woman scored 98. However, the woman was declared the winner. Why?

Clues: 103; Answers: 147

Poor Investment

A man bought a house for $1,000,000 as an investment. The house was well kept and carefully maintained by a good caretaker. Although the house remained in perfect structural order, within a few years it was worthless. Why?

Clues: 103; Answer: 147

Give Us a Hand ...

A man searching for precious stones didn't find any, but found a severed human hand instead. What had happened?

Clues: 103; Answer: 147

Evil Intent

A rich man meets a lady at the theater and invites her back to his house for a drink. She has a drink and then leaves. About an hour later he suddenly realizes that she intends to return and burgle his house. How does he know?

Clues: 103;
Answer: 148

Two Heads Are Better Than One!

Several Americans reported they saw a creature that had two heads, two arms, and four legs. They were surprised, frightened, and alarmed, and when they told their friends, nobody believed them. But they were reliable witnesses. What had they seen?

Clues: 104; Answer: 148

Stone Me!

A boy flung a stone at a man and many people's lives were saved. How come?

Clues: 104; Answer: 148

Judge for Yourself

The defendant in a major lawsuit asked his lawyer if he should send the judge a box of fine cigars in the hope of influencing him. The lawyer said it was a very bad idea and would prejudice the judge against him. The defendant listened carefully, sent the cigars, and won the case. What happened?

Clues: 104; Answer: 149

Love Letters

Why did a woman send out 1,000 anonymous Valentine's cards to different men?

Clues: 104; Answer: 149

Strange Behavior

A man was driving down the road into town with his family on a clear day. He saw a tree and immediately stopped the car and then reversed at high speed. Why?

Clues: 104; Answer: 149

Tree Trouble

The authorities were concerned that a famous old tree was being damaged because so many tourists came up to it and touched it. So a wall was built around the tree to protect it. But this had the opposite effect of that intended. Why?

Clues: 105; Answer: 149

The Burial Chamber

Why did a man build a beautiful burial chamber, complete with sculptures and paintings, and then deliberately wreck it?

Clues: 105; Answer: 149

Miscarriage of Justice

An Italian judge released a guilty man and convicted an innocent man and as a result the confectionery industry has greatly benefited. Why?

Clues: 105; Answer: 150

Offenses Down

The police in Sussex, England, found a new way to complete their form-filling and paperwork that significantly reduced crime. What was it?

Clues: 105; Answer: 150

Police Chase

A high-speed police car chases a much slower vehicle in which criminals are escaping. But the police fail to catch them. Why?

Clues: 106; Answer: 151

Café Society

A mall café is pestered by teenagers who come in, buy a single cup of coffee, and stay for hours, and thus cut down on available space for other customers. How does the owner get rid of them, quite legally?

Clues: 106; Answer: 151

Hi, Jean!

A shop owner introduced expensive new procedures to make his premises more hygienic, but the results were the very opposite. Why?

Clues: 106; Answer: 151

The Empty Machine

A gumball machine dispensed gum when quarters were inserted. When the machine was opened, there was no money inside. A considerable number of gumballs had been consumed and the machine did not appear to have been interfered with in any way. What had happened?

Clues: 106;
Answer: 151

Take a Fence

A man painted his garden fence green and then went on holiday. When he came back two weeks later, he was amazed to see that the fence was blue. Nobody had touched the fence. What had happened?

Clues: 107; Answer: 151

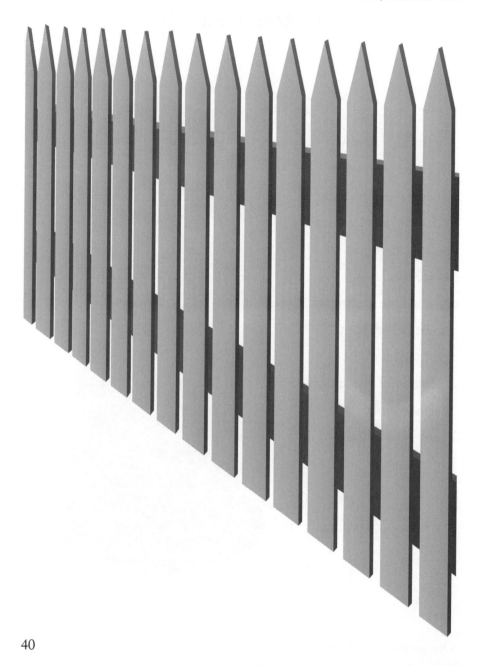

Wally Test II

Time for another WALLY Test. The questions may look easy, but be warned—they're designed to trip you up. Write down your answers on a piece of paper and then see how many you got right. The time limit is three minutes.

1. What should you give an injured lemon?
2. If an atheist died in church, what would they put on his coffin?
3. Who went into the lion's den unarmed and came out alive?
4. A man rode down the street on a horse, yet walked. How come?
5. How can you eat an egg without breaking the shell?
6. Why was King Henry VIII buried in Westminster Abbey?
7. In China they hang many criminals, but they will not hang a man with a wooden leg. Why?
8. Why do storks stand on one leg?
9. A circular field is covered in thick snow. A black cow with white spots is in the middle. Two white cows with black spots are on the edge of the field. What time is it?
10. What was the problem with the wooden car with wooden wheels and a wooden engine?

Answers: 190

Sex Discrimination

When lawyers went to prison to visit their clients they found that female lawyers were searched on entry but male lawyers were not. Why?

Clues: 107; Answer: 152

Weight Loss

How did a Japanese diet clinic achieve great weight-loss results for its patients even though they did not change their diet or undertake more activity than normal?

Clues: 107; Answer: 152

Psychic

You enter a parking lot and see a woman walking toward you. You then see a row of cars and know immediately which one is hers. How?

Clues: 107; Answer: 152

The Happy Robber

A robber holds up a bank, but leaves with no money whatsoever. However, he is more pleased than if he had left with lots of money. Why?

Clues: 108; Answer: 152

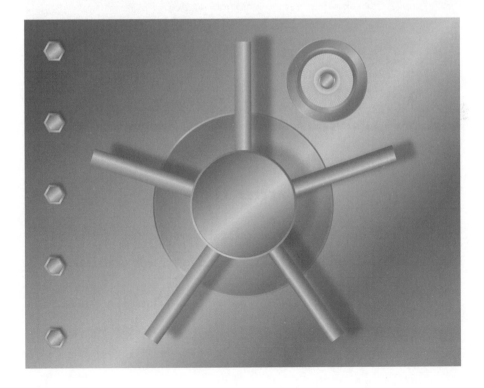

Siege Mentality

A city is under siege. The attackers have run out of ammunition and have suffered heavy casualties. Yet they take the city within a few days without further losses. How?

Clues: 108; Answer: 152

Carrier Bags

During World War II, the British Royal Navy had very few aircraft carriers. What ingenious plan was devised to remedy this deficiency?

Clues: 108; Answer: 153

The Cathedral Untouched

When London was bombed during World War II, St. Paul's Cathedral, in the center of the city, was never hit. Why not?

Clues: 108; Answer: 153

Bags Away

An airplane nearly crashed because one of the passengers had not fastened his suitcase securely enough. What happened?

Clues: 109; Answer: 153

The Sad Samaritan

Jim saw a stranded motorist on a country road. The motorist had run out of fuel, so Jim took him to the nearest garage and then drove him back to his car. Jim felt good that he had been such a good Samaritan, but discovered something later that made him very sad. What was it?

Clues: 109; Answer: 154

The Tallest Tree

Men found what they suspected was the tallest tree in Australia. It was growing in the outback in rough terrain and with other trees around. They did not have any advanced instruments with them. How did they accurately measure the height of the tree?

Clues: 109; Answer: 154

The Unwelcome Guest

A couple had a neighbor who continually arrived at mealtimes in the hope of getting a free meal. How did they use their very friendly dog to persuade the neighbor not to come for free meals again?

Clues: 109; Answer: 154

Poor Show

Every time he performed in public, it was a complete flop. Yet he became famous for it, and won medals and prizes. People came from all over and paid to see him perform. Who was he?

Clues: 110; Answer: 155

Message Received

How did Alexander the Great send secret messages with his envoy?

Clues: 110; Answer: 155

The Mighty Stone

There was a huge boulder in the middle of a village green. It was too big to be moved, too hard to split, and dynamiting it was too dangerous. How did a simple peasant suggest getting rid of it?

Clues: 110; Answer: 155

The World's Most Expensive Car

The most expensive car ever made is for sale. Although many people want to own it and can afford to buy it, nobody will do so. Why?

Clues: 111; Answer: 155

The Fatal Fall

A woman dropped a piece of wood. She picked it up again and carried on as if nothing had happened. The wood was not damaged and she was not injured, but the incident cost her her life. Why?

Clues: 111; Answer: 156

Election Selection

There is an election in a deprived city area. All the political parties put up candidates, actively canvass, and spend money on their campaigns. Yet the election is won by a candidate who did not canvass or advertise and is unknown to all of the electors. How?

Clues: 112; Answer: 156

Well Trained

A man, a woman, and a child are watching a train come into a station. "Here it comes," says the man. "Here she comes," says the woman. "Here he comes," says the child. Who was correct?

Clues: 112;
Answer: 156

Razor Attack

A man had his throat attacked by a woman with a razor, yet he suffered no serious injuries. How come?

Clues: 112; Answer: 156

The Old Crooner

How did Bing Crosby reduce the crime rate in various U.S. cities?

Clues: 112; Answer: 156

Generosity?

A man took considerable trouble to acquire some money, but then quickly gave most of it away. Why?

Clues: 113; Answer: 157

The Parson's Pup

Why did the vicar want only a black dog?

Clues: 113; Answer: 157

Watch That Man!

A runner was awarded a prize for winning a marathon. But the judges disqualified him when they saw a picture of his wristwatch. Why?

Clues: 113; Answer: 158

Quarters

A man and his wife are dead. If the man had had just one quarter, his wife would have lived. If he had had two quarters, he would have lived. If he had had three quarters, both the man and his wife would have lived, but his brother would have died. Why?

Clues: 113; Answer: 158

Oskar

Oskar Kokoschka, an Austrian abstract expressionist painter, arrived in England in 1938, after having escaped from the Nazi terror in Europe. Kokoschka was an artist and had never been a politician, yet he blamed himself for the dangerous state that Europe was in, and later for the catastrophe of World War II. Why?

Clues: 114; Answer: 159

Drink and Die I

On a very dark night, a man was outside walking. When he came around a corner, he saw a building on which were written the words "Drink and Die." What did it mean?

Clues: 114; Answer: 159

Drink and Die II

Two men wearing helmets drank some cool beer and then died. If they had drunk warm beer, they would have lived. What happened?

Clues: 114; Answer: 159

Traffic Offense

A man goes to work in the same manner every working day for twenty years. However, one morning going to work in the same way, he is arrested by the police. Why?

Clues: 114; Answer: 159

Bad Bump

Julie bumped into George and they both died. Why?

Clues: 115; Answer: 160

The Clever Detective

When the detective arrived at the scene of the crime, he had no idea who the criminal was. He turned to his assistant and said: "We are looking for someone with the initials A and S." How did he know?

Clues: 115; Answer: 160

The Silent Robber

The manager of a factory was very concerned to learn that valuable copper had gone missing again during the night. The security guards assured him that the security was very tight and no one could have gotten in or out of the factory. What was happening?

Clues: 115; Answer: 160

A Difference in Attitude

The driver of an underground train made an announcement that infuriated some of his passengers and amused the other passengers. What was it?

Clues: 115; Answer: 161

Insecure

A new, seemingly superior security device for houses is marketed. However, in practice, it turns out to be inferior to existing, conventional systems. Why?

Clues: 116; Answer: 161

Deadly Talk

The speech killed the President. How come?

Clues: 116; Answer: 162

The Fruit of Sarcasm

What he had intended to be a sarcastic statement resulted in an invention that's now in common use. What is it?

Clues: 116; Answer: 162

Timepiece

Why are most watches shown in magazines fixed at the time ten to two or ten past ten?

Clues: 116; Answer: 163

Racing Certainty

In an international 100-meter sprint race, the athlete who ran the 100 meters in the fastest time was not the winner of the race. Why?

Clues: 117;
Answer: 163

No Claims Bonus

A stuntman has to insure himself every time he jumps from a height. He does this and performs the jump, but something goes wrong and he is crippled for life. The insurance company refuses to pay out. Why?

Clues: 117; Answer: 163

Second of One

They had no one to beat but came in second. How come?

Clues: 117; Answer: 164

Death by Reading

She died because she was a voracious reader. How come?

Clues: 117; Answer: 164

My Condiments to the Chef

It is possible to buy wine flavored with salt and pepper to use in cooking. But since you can always add salt and pepper to table wine, why does anybody bother to produce cooking wine?

Clues: 118; Answer: 164

Elementary

When she saw the fishing boat in the far distance, she knew that it had already hauled in its catch. How did she know?

Clues: 118; Answer: 165

Taking the Right Steps

Two men carried a ladder that was 18 feet (5.4 m) long down a corridor in a hotel. The corridor was 8 feet (2.4 m) high and 6 feet (1.8 m) wide. They came to a T-shape junction with another corridor of the same dimensions in the same building. There were no windows or doors they could use, and the ladder was one single piece with no joints. How did they get the ladder around the bend?

Clues: 118; Answer: 165

Only in the U.S.A.

On the fourteenth of March each year in the United States, there is a certain celebration that does not take place in Europe. In fact, this celebration would never take place in Europe. Why?

Clues: 119; Answer: 165

Cheaper by the Dozen

The more gas I use, the lower the bill from my gas supplier. Why?

Clues: 119; Answer: 166

Lakeless

A man in the woods came to a place where he knew a small lake had been. When he found that the lake was not there, he knew that he was in mortal danger. Why?

Clues: 119; Answer: 166

Red-Faced

A man who received a signed copy of a book in the mail was severely embarrassed. Why?

Clues: 119; Answer: 167

Picture Book

Why did this weatherman draw a little picture of a ship on a map of the Atlantic Ocean?

Clues: 120; Answer: 167

Poor Pet

Despite the fact that it involved the unfortunate death of an animal, it was hailed as one of the greatest human achievements of all time. What was it?

Clues: 120; Answer: 168

High Flyer

A man who was boarding a plane was severely embarrassed when the airplane's engines started. Why?

Clues: 120; Answer: 168

Birds of a Feather

Why does a flock of birds fly in a V-shape formation?

Clues: 120; Answer: 168

Deadly Delivery

A man was killed, and as a result, the post office has had to deliver millions more pieces of mail. Who was he?

Clues: 120; Answer: 169

Fatal Fork

A man went to work carrying a fork and a net. Another man died. How?

Clues: 121; Answer: 169

Groovy Movie

A famous director came to Ireland to make a film. Many local people thought that they would be able to get jobs as extras. They were surprised at the criteria the director had for selecting local extras. What was he looking for?

Clues: 121; Answer: 170

Double Your Money

Why does a man cut all his banknotes in two?

Clues: 121; Answer: 170

Malfunction

A man had a piece of machinery that was not working. So he opened it up and discovered a 2-inch (5-cm) moth flying around inside the machine. He took the moth out, cleaned the machine, and found that it worked very well. His actions have given us a useful new phrase in the modern English language. What is the phrase?

Clues: 121; Answer: 170

A Friendly Match?

After a friendly football game, the two teams shook hands and then tried to kill each other. Why?

Clues: 121; Answer: 171

Lifesaver

A man held a newspaper very close to his chest in order to save his life. How?

Clues: 122; Answer: 171

The Plant

Why does a policeman put a plastic bag of talcum powder in a woman's coat pocket?

Clues: 122; Answer: 171

Memory Transplant

A man was so forgetful that he needed an operation. What was it for?

Clues: 122; Answer: 172

The Kitty's Ming

Why does a man feed his cat using a very valuable Ming bowl?

Clues: 122; Answer: 172

Stranger Danger

A stranger came to the house. No one had seen him before. He stayed just one week, did not say a word, and then left. Everyone was sad when he went. Who was he?

Clues: 123; Answer: 173

WALLY Test III

Ready for another WALLY test? I thought so. These are the sort of questions that are meant to cause you consternation, so take your best shot and see how close you get to the right answer. Try to answer all the question in three minutes or less.

1. What kind of men can never die of old age?
2. What three-letter word completes the first word and starts the second?

   DON CAR
3. A man owed a huge amount of money. He paid half of it. How much does he owe now?
4. What sort of fur do you get from a tiger?
5. Where are the Pyrenees?
6. Who was the tallest president of the United States?
7. What does a duck do if it flies upside down?
8. Why was the postman unlucky?
9. Who are the most dependable staff in a hospital?

Answers: 191

The Lethal Lie

A man was captured and interrogated. His captors tell him, truthfully, that if he answers their questions truthfully, his life will be spared. Although he answers their questions truthfully, they immediately shoot him dead. Why?

Clues: 123; Answer: 173

Focus Pocus

A very precious jewel is on display at an exhibition. A guard is hired to protect it for an hour and promises not to take his eyes off it for that period. However, at the end of the hour, the jewel is examined and found to be a fake. At the beginning of the hour, it was genuine. The guard swears that he never took his eyes off the jewel during the hour, and he is an honest man. What had happened?

Clues: 123; Answer: 174

Outrage

Who were the first couple to appear on prime-time television in bed together?

Clues: 123; Answer: 174

First Time, Last Time

A dancer performed a dance in front of a large audience. It was a dance he had never rehearsed. What was going on?

Clues: 124; Answer: 174

Speechless

Pierre was a healthy young man. He had not seen his friends or family for a while. Then something happened. When he saw his friends and family, he could not speak to them. Why?

Clues: 124; Answer: 175

Meeting and Greeting

A woman was hurrying down a street when she met an old friend she had not seen for many years. She did not shake hands or wave to her friend. Why not?

Clues: 124; Answer: 175

Playacting

A rich man wrote a bad play and paid a producer a lot of money in return for his promise to put it on stage for him as part of a theatrical evening. The producer did this, but when the playwright attended the opening performance, he was very angry. Why?

Clues: 124; Answer: 175

The Uneaten

A little boy and girl were thrilled when their father gave them Easter eggs. But they never ate them—why not?

Clues: 125; Answer: 176

Walk of Death

A woman went out for a walk on a summer's day. She was later found dead with severe head injuries. The police fail to find any murder weapon. How did she die?

Clues: 125; Answer:176

Defensive Measure

Security firms used to advise clients who wanted to protect their houses to build high walls around them to keep out burglars and other intruders. Now they simply recommend fences. The walls and fences were equally difficult to scale. So why switch to fences?

Clues: 125; Answer: 176

Shaping the World

Why did a former world leader copyright a strange shape?

Clues: 125; Answer: 177

The Shot That Saved

A woman took a photo of her son that saved his life. How?

Clues: 125; Answer: 177

False Confession

Why did a man call the police and tell them that he had shot someone when he had not?

Clues: 126; Answer: 178

Garment for Rent

Why did a man destroy the sweater that his wife had made for him?

Clues: 126; Answer: 178

Key Decision

A man wishes to enter a building, so he acquires a key to the front door of the building. It is the correct key that fits and would indeed open the lock. However, when he tries to enter the building, he finds that he cannot. There is no other person or guard dog around, and no other lock, bolt, or restraint on the door. Why can he not gain entry to the building?

Clues: 126; Answer: 179

A Long Way to Go for a Drink

A man travels to another country in order to have a drink in a bar. He could have had the same drink in a bar in his home country. Why did he travel?

Clues: 126; Answer: 179

Pop the Question

A man proposed to a woman. She promised she would give him her answer at dinner the following week. After they had dinner, she said, "Do you want my answer?" He replied, "I know it already." How did he know?

Clues: 127; Answer: 180

Custom and Practice

Mark Twain was stopped by Customs and asked what he had in his suitcase. He replied, "Just clothes." However, when the official searched his suitcase, he found a large bottle of whisky on which Twain would have to pay duty. What explanation did Twain give that caused the official to smile and let him through without payment?

Clues: 127; Answer: 180

Towitt, Towoo

A man walking through a small forest finds a stuffed owl perched on a branch of a tree. Why is the stuffed owl there?

Clues: 127; Answer: 180

Plane Puzzler

A plane flying at 25,000 feet (7,500 meters) suddenly switches off all its engines but is in no danger. Why?

Clues: 127; Answer: 181

High Caliber

A man was shot many times and lived. His wife was shot just once and died. How come?

Clues: 128; Answer: 181

Wounded Enemy

A man shoots his enemy and wounds him severely, but he's careful not to kill him. Why?

Clues: 128; Answer: 181

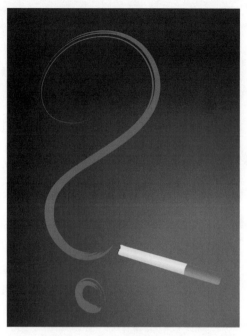

Smoking Is Bad for You

A man comes home and finds his wife smoking a cigarette. No word is exchanged between them. The man goes over to a broom closet, hauls another man out of it, and flattens him with a punch. The husband and wife smile and embrace each other. What is going on?

Clues: 128; Answer: 182

Determined to Die

Jacques was determined to commit suicide. He stood on top of a seaside cliff and tied a noose around his neck and tied the other end of the rope to a large rock. Then Jacques drank poison and set fire to his clothes. He had a gun ready to shoot himself. He jumped from the cliff and fired the pistol. What happened?

Clues: 128; Answer: 182

Hello, Grandma!

When her grandmother dropped in to visit her at her office, a woman was severely embarrassed. Why?

Clues: 128; Answer: 183

Cake Killer

A woman ate a slice of cake with her fingers. Afterwards she did not wash her hands. As a result of this, she died a few hours later. Why?

Clues: 129; Answer: 183

Vacation, Vacation, Vacation

Why does a major bank insist that all its employees take two weeks' vacation in one stretch? It has nothing to do with the welfare of the employees.

Clues: 129; Answer: 184

Clerical Advantage

Bishops could have seven. Priests could have five. Ordinary people could only have one. What is it?

Clues: 129; Answer: 184

Bad Loser

A man playing in the final round of a tough competition loses. In a fit of anger, he shoots the winner with a gun with the result that his opponent can never play again. However, the police are not called, and the man escapes with a fine and a simple warning. Why?

Clues: 129; Answer: 184

Puppy Love

Children got into trouble because of a dog, which was well trained and very well behaved. Why?

Clues: 130; Answer: 185

A woman dialed 911 to ask for help. She was told not to open her door but to open her window. She first tried to open the window, and then the door. She died. Why?

Clues: 130; Answer: 185

The Lethal Warning

A man died because he warned his friend of danger. How?

Clues: 130; Answer: 186

Field of Gold

Why did a farmer spray his field with golden dye?

Clues: 130; Answer: 186

Good Bump

A woman driver usually slowed down when approaching a speed bump in the road, but one day she accelerated toward one and drove over it quite quickly. Why?

Clues: 131; Answer: 186

Timeless

Which woman has appeared most often on the cover of Time magazine?

Clues: 131; Answer: 187

Chilly

What desert is the coldest on Earth and why?

Clues: 131; Answer: 187

The Silly Salesman

A salesman died because he was preparing for his sales call. How?

Clues: 131; Answer: 187

It's Not True!

Why did the teacher write this on the blackboard: "Woman without her man is helpless"?

Clues: 131; Answer: 188

Not Here, Son

A schoolboy was an avid athlete. The police in the village where he lived stopped him from practicing athletic feats. Why?

Clues: 131; Answer: 188

Unsanitary Janitor

Why did the janitor dip his mop in the toilet before cleaning the bathroom mirror?

Clues: 132; Answer: 189

Hyper-Inflation

Why did a bottle of wine jump in value a thousandfold overnight?

Clues: 132; Answer: 189

WALLY Test IV

Here's a final WALLY Test for you to try. These are some sneaky questions, so don't feel too bad if you get some of them wrong. Who knows? Maybe you'll get every single one right—grab a pencil and a stopwatch to find out. You have three minutes to write down all of your answers.

1. How can a boy switch off the light that's 10 feet (about 3 meters) from his bed and get into bed before it is dark?
2. You're standing in line at the ticket desk at an airport. The man in front of you is going to New York. The woman behind you is going to London. Where are you going?
3. Who are always after you?
4. If a cat can kill a rat in two minutes, how long would it take a cat to kill 100 rats?
5. What can move and be still at the same time?
6. Why does a postman call his bag John and not Jane?
7. What kind of rocks are found just below the surface of Lake Superior?
8. February is the shortest month; what is the longest month?
9. Where are the best parties on a cruise ship?

Answers: 191

THE CLUES

The Deadly Sculpture

✓ He lived a lonely life in a remote building.

✓ He made the statue out of copper. It was taken far away and he never saw it again.

✓ He died as the result of an accident. No other person or animal or sculpture was involved.

Peak Performance

✓ He had been dead for many years, so it was not possible to tell from his physical condition or clothing whether he had reached the summit.

✓ The manner of his death is not relevant.

✓ No camera was involved.

✓ What would he have done had he reached the summit?

The Fatal Fish

✓ The man died in an accident. He was not poisoned or stabbed.

✓ No other person was involved. No crime was involved.

✓ The man did not eat the fish. The type of fish is irrelevant. It was dead.

✓ He was not indoors.

Adam Had None

✓ It has nothing to do with family, relations, bones, or physical appearance.

✓ It has to do with names.

Shot Dead

✓ The woman and the strangers were neither criminals nor police.

✓ The strangers did not see the woman and did not know that she was in the house.

✓ The strangers were armed and were a threat to the woman.

Would You Believe It?

✓ The blocks of wood were identical and so were the people (for the purposes of this puzzle), but their circumstances were not identical.

✓ Normal forces were at work in all three cases—nothing unusual was going on.

Jailbreak

✓ There was an advantage to him in escaping in the morning. It had nothing to do with light, or deliveries, or prison officer routines.

✓ He did not want to be spotted once he was outside the prison.

✓ He knew that his escape would be detected after about half an hour.

Sitting Ducks

✓ The woman loves animals and hates hunting. She does not intend to use the gun for hunting or for self-defense.

✓ There is no criminal intent in mind.

✓ The ducks are already dead when she shoots them.

Bald Facts

✓ Mary, Queen of Scots took great care never to be seen without her wig.

✓ Her wig was very good and looked completely natural.

✓ Although Mary, Queen of Scots never wanted to be seen without her wig, she was not upset or embarrassed when it eventually happened, even though many people saw it.

Lethal Action

✓ The dead people were Africans. They didn't eat the fruit.

✓ The Brazilian authorities' actions involved pesticides.

✓ The Africans acted illegally. Their deaths were accidents.

Recognition

✓ His Aunt Mary was not carrying a sign or wearing anything distinctive. She did not have any disabilities or characteristics that would make her stand out.

✓ He had not arranged to meet her in a specific place or asked her to wear or carry anything in particular.

✓ He recognized her from her facial appearance.

Destruction

✓ The customer was a man who accidentally destroyed the premises without knowing that he was doing so.

✓ He was there the whole time that the premises were being destroyed.

✓ He was very overweight.

Pesky Escalator

✓ There was no one else around.

✓ The foreign visitor saw a sign.

✓ He was very obedient.

Wonderful Walk

✓ Something annoying happened during the walk in the woods.

✓ It gave the man an idea.

✓ He invented a popular fastener.

Poles Apart

✓ The explorers knew that there would be no sources of food other than what they carried with them.

✓ They did something that would not normally be considered a good idea.

Arrested Development

✓ The robber wanted to get out of the bank as quickly as he could.

✓ There was nothing particularly noticeable or remarkable about the bank robber that would make him easy to identify.

✓ He was not very bright.

Holed Out

✓ It was not a good shot that got him the hole in one.

✓ He should have been more careful.

✓ The golfer's ball rebounded into the hole.

✓ Another person was involved.

Trunk-ated

✓ The policeman is able to prove that there is something suspicious in the trunk without opening it.

✓ He suspects that there is a body in the trunk.

Sports Mad

✓ The sports fan was not exercising. He was not injured. He wanted the tape because of his sports obsession.

✓ No sports equipment is involved.

✓ He was a football fan. He followed his team fanatically but rarely got the chance to go to the games.

Appendectomy I & II

✓ No financial gain is involved in either solution.

✓ The doctors who removed the healthy appendixes acted out of good motives.

✓ Both solutions involve situations in the first part of the 20th century.

Riotous Assembly

✓ The section did not have the equipment it needed to reopen.

✓ The rioters had used everything they could lay their hands on.

✓ The police had intervened but were driven back when the rioters threw rocks at them.

Kneed to Know

✓ The man and his wife were in a room full of people.
✓ She put her hand on his knee not as a sign of affection or encouragement but as an act of communication.
✓ He gained an understanding through her actions.

Bad Trip

✓ The anti-drug agency wanted to actively promote a message that drugs were bad, but inadvertently they ended up promoting the opposite message.
✓ The agency distributed pencils to children and the children used them.

Two Letters

✓ He is not trying to form words or to communicate or send a message.
✓ The man is working on a crossword puzzle.
✓ The letters he writes are S and E.

Body of Evidence

✓ The woman was seen entering and leaving the police station, but no one tried to stop her.
✓ She was not a criminal or deliberately aiding a criminal.
✓ She was doing her job.

Shakespeare's Blunder

✓ The blunder did not involve physics, chemistry, mathematics, or astronomy.

✓ The blunder concerned the twins, Viola and Sebastian.

No Charge

✓ The arresting officer followed the correct procedure and read the man his rights. There was clear evidence of his crime. But his lawyer got him released on a clear breach of his rights.

✓ The crime he committed is irrelevant.

✓ He did not own any music CDs or radios.

Pond Life

✓ The same environmental change would have occurred if felt hats or woolen hats had become very popular.

✓ More silk hats were sold and fewer other hats were sold.

✓ Fur hats were out of fashion.

Shoe Shop Shuffle

✓ The four shops have similar staffing, lighting, and security arrangements.

✓ The shop that suffers the heaviest thefts is not in a worse part of town or in an environment that is more popular with criminals.

✓ The shop that suffers the heaviest thefts does something different with its shoes.

Caesar's Blunder

✓ The sea was calm and there were no storms when Caesar sailed across the channel and arrived in Britain.

✓ He arrived safely and disembarked his troops and equipment.

✓ Caesar had never visited Britain before.

✓ He had learned to sail in the Mediterranean.

Slow Death

✓ Aeschylus did not trip over the tortoise or slip on it.

✓ He did not eat it or attempt to eat it. He was not poisoned or bitten by the tortoise.

✓ No other human was involved in his death.

Driving Away

✓ Driving conditions were excellent, but the thief found the woman's car very difficult to drive.

✓ She had had the car modified.

✓ The rich woman suffered from some of the same frailties as other old people.

✓ There was nothing unusual about the car's engine, gears, wheels, steering, or bodywork.

Lit Too Well?

✓ The authorities deliberately set up lights in fields and on roads even though people living there had not requested them and did not need them.

✓ There was damage to fields, crops, roads, and farm animals as a result.

✓ Overall, though, human lives were saved.

Quick on the Draw

✓ He had a perfectly valid ticket for that day's lottery, but he was not a prizewinner.

✓ He saw the exact numbers on his ticket come up on the TV show.

✓ He had a cruel wife.

Scaled Down

✓ The butcher had only one turkey left.

✓ He weighed it for the customer.

✓ He pressed down on the scale with his thumb in order to give it an exaggerated weight.

The Happy Woman

✓ Although she used a driver, she walked about four miles in the course of her tour.

✓ She wore special shoes.

✓ She saw many flags.

Vandal Scandal

✓ The authorities did not add extra security or protection for the ancient buildings.

✓ They fooled the people who were determined to take souvenirs.

✓ Tourists went away happy.

The Deadly Drawing

✓ She was correct in her deduction that someone had been killed.

✓ She did not know the person who had been killed, nor who had killed them, nor how they had died.

✓ She had never been in that room before and she had not seen the picture before.

Leonardo's Secret

✓ Leonardo hid the designs in a place where he thought nobody would ever find them, but they were not buried or locked away.

✓ People carefully stored the hidden designs for years without realizing they had them.

Down Periscope

✓ The submarine was in water at all times and was not on dry ground or in dry dock.

✓ No water entered the submarine.

✓ This could happen only in certain places, and not in the open sea.

The Letter Left Out

✓ The letter that is left out is chosen not because it is rarely used but because it is easily substituted without any risk of misunderstanding.

Arrested Development—Again

✓ The robbers wore masks so as not to be recognized.
✓ They made a clean getaway.
✓ Bank employees noticed something about the two men.
✓ The men were brothers.

Titanic Proportions

✓ The ship that sank was not involved in the sinking of the Titanic or the rescue operation.
✓ Laws were passed to ensure that ships improved their safety.
✓ One ship sank but all the passengers were saved.

The Mover

✓ It is something you see every day.
✓ In fact you have seen one in the last few seconds.

Death of a Player

✓ The man was not involved in any collisions or tackles and did not suffer any injuries, yet it was because of his sport that he accidentally died.

✓ He was a golfer, but he was not hit by a club or a ball or indeed by anything.

✓ If only he had put his tee in his pocket!

Hot Picture

✓ She loved the picture, but she deliberately had it burned. No trace of it was left.

✓ There was no criminal intent on her part, and she did not make any financial gains.

✓ The picture was a present.

✓ Her husband was a motorcyclist.

Genuine Article

✓ The play was written by Shakespeare and this was proven beyond doubt.

✓ It had been copied and written out on a computer, so there were no clues from the paper or handwriting.

✓ No analysis of the style or content was needed to prove its authenticity.

Unhealthy Lifestyle

✓ The man's unhealthy habits helped save him.

✓ No other people were involved.

✓ The woman died from poison.

New World Record

✓ She did not do anything physical.

✓ She became the only known person to achieve a certain feat.

✓ It was not her age alone that did this, though one would have to be old to do it.

Death by Romance

✓ They did not die of food or gas poisoning, nor from the effects of any kind of exertion.

✓ They were not murdered. They died by accident.

✓ They were in an unusual house.

Penalty

✓ It was a regular soccer match played in the World Cup in front of thousands of people.

✓ The players were not criminals or terrorists—just soccer players.

✓ The match was played in an Arab country.

Golf Challenge I, II, & III

✓ I. The woman's gender was no handicap.

✓ II. The woman was more than a match for the man.

✓ III. It was a very wet day and the golf course was flooded.

Poor Investment

✓ There were no other buildings nearby, and no buildings or roads were added or removed in the vicinity.

✓ There were no earthquakes, floods, fires, or eruptions, and no damage by trees or vegetation.

✓ The house had a beautiful view.

Give Us a Hand ...

✓ The man whose hand it was had also been looking for precious stones.

✓ He had been forced to cut off his own hand.

✓ To find these precious stones, men needed strong limbs, good eyes, good lungs, and great fitness.

Evil Intent

✓ It was nothing she said or did with the man. He did not remember anything to cause his realization that she planned to burgle him.

✓ He noticed something.

✓ While he was preparing the drinks, she did something.

✓ He had his hands full.

Two Heads Are Better Than One!

✓ They were not drunk or under any strange influence.

✓ This happened in North America.

✓ They had seen a creature they had never seen before.

Stone Me!

✓ The man was much bigger than the boy.

✓ The stone hit the man on the head.

✓ Many people watched.

Judge for Yourself

✓ The defendant's actions probably influenced the judge in his favor.

✓ The judge was scrupulously honest and would resent any intent to bribe or influence him.

Love Letters

✓ She didn't know the men and didn't like any of them.

✓ She had malicious intentions.

✓ There was potential financial gain for her.

Strange Behavior

✓ There were many trees along the side of the road. The man had never seen or noticed this tree before.

✓ There was something different about this tree.

✓ His primary concern was safety.

✓ The tree itself was not a threat to him.

Tree Trouble

✓ The wall was successful in keeping prying people away from the tree—just as intended.

✓ The tree died.

The Burial Chamber

✓ The burial chamber wasn't built for use by the builder.

✓ He wrecked it before anyone was buried there.

✓ He did not wreck it out of spite or anger. He deliberately destroyed it in order to deceive.

✓ He wrecked the chamber in order to save the chamber.

Miscarriage of Justice

✓ The Italian judge tried a rebel, but released a robber.

✓ The Italian was not in Italy when he made the judgment.

✓ The judge, the rebel, and the robber never ate any chocolate.

Offenses Down

✓ The police officers filled in their reports and forms in a different fashion, which reduced crime, but they did not fill them in any better or quicker or more accurately or with more information than before.

✓ They filled in the reports by hand, not by computer.

✓ The key difference was their location when they did the paperwork.

Police Chase

✓ The fast police car was right behind the criminals' vehicle and there was no other traffic or vehicle involved. The roads were clear and the weather was fine.

✓ The getaway vehicle was a bus.

✓ The bus driver was number seven.

Café Society

✓ The café owner did not change the menu or prices or music in the café.

✓ He changed the appearance of the café in a way that embarrassed the teenagers.

Hi, Jean!

✓ The shop owner sold food and he wanted to present it in the best possible light.

✓ He took action to deter and kill pests.

The Empty Machine

✓ Kids had cheated the gum company.

✓ They had not put quarters into the machine, but they had obtained gumballs.

✓ The machine was rusty, but it still worked fine.

Take a Fence

✓ No other person or animal was involved.

✓ The change in color was not caused by the sun or wind.

✓ The change in color was caused by the rain, but every other house and fence in the area remained unchanged in color.

Sex Discrimination

✓ The prison guards were not acting in a discriminatory, sexist, or unfair fashion, but simply following procedures.

✓ Women were more likely to fall afoul of the security equipment.

Weight Loss

✓ The diet and the daily regimen were not changed. But something else about the clinic was changed, and this produced the weight loss in patients.

✓ The change made the patients work a little harder in normal activities.

✓ The fact that the clinic is in Japan is not particularly relevant. Similar results could have been obtained in many countries—but not in Belgium or Holland.

Psychic

✓ You see the cars after you see the woman, and you did not see her leaving the car.

✓ There is something different in the appearance of her car.

✓ She is carrying something.

The Happy Robber

✓ He was poor. He stole something from the bank, but it was not money.

✓ He made no financial gain from the theft. He stole for love.

✓ He stole a rare liquid.

Siege Mentality

✓ This took place in the Middle Ages.

✓ The defenders had plenty of food, water, and ammunition.

✓ The attackers had catapulted rocks over the walls, but had now run out of ammunition.

Carrier Bags

✓ The suggestion was a way of creating new aircraft carriers much more cheaply than by the conventional methods.

✓ It would possibly have been practical in the North Atlantic.

✓ They were disposable carriers.

The Cathedral Untouched

✓ The area all around St. Paul's was heavily bombed, but it appeared that no bombs could fall on St. Paul's.

✓ The German bombers deliberately avoided bombing it.

✓ They were not acting out of any religious or moral principles.

Bags Away

✓ The passenger's suitcase was stored in the hold of the plane.

✓ He was not a terrorist or criminal.

✓ The passenger's suitcase did not contain chemicals, explosives, or drugs.

The Sad Samaritan

✓ Jim was not robbed or deceived by the motorist in any way.

✓ Jim tried his best to help, but failed.

✓ The motorist was stranded.

The Tallest Tree

✓ The men did not use angles or shadows.

✓ They did not climb the tree.

✓ They measured it accurately using rope and measuring lines.

✓ How do you attempt to contact a dead man?

The Unwelcome Guest

✓ The neighbor liked the dog and the dog did not annoy the neighbor.

✓ The couple gave the neighbor a fine meal.

✓ He was horrified at what happened next.

Poor Show

✓ His performances were always a flop, but he was very successful.

✓ He was not in comedy, music, cinema, or theater.

✓ His most famous performance was in Mexico.

✓ He was a sportsman.

Message Received

✓ Envoys were thoroughly searched when they arrived at a foreign location to check for hidden messages.

✓ The envoys did not memorize the messages or ever know or see the contents of the messages.

✓ The messages were hidden on the person of the envoy but they could not be seen, even when the envoy was naked.

The Mighty Stone

✓ The peasant did not suggest building over it.

✓ He suggested a way of moving the stone, but not by pushing it or pulling it.

✓ He used its own weight to help move it.

The World's Most Expensive Car

✓ The car was used once and is in good condition, but it has not been driven for many years.

✓ Most people have seen it on TV, but they can't name the man who drove it.

✓ It is not associated with any celebrity or with any remarkable historical event or tragedy, though when it was driven it was a special event at the time.

✓ It was developed at great expense for practical use and not for show or exhibition.

The Fatal Fall

✓ The woman wasn't a criminal, and no crime was involved.

✓ She was quite upset to have dropped the piece of wood.

✓ The wood was a cylinder about one foot long.

✓ The piece of wood was not particularly valuable and could easily be replaced.

✓ Many people saw her drop the piece of wood.

Election Selection

✓ The successful candidate had no particular experience, qualifications, or characteristics that qualified him for the job or increased his appeal to voters.

✓ He did not canvass or advertise or spend money in any way to influence the voters, and he remained unknown to the voters.

✓ The other candidates were competent and trustworthy and did nothing to disqualify themselves.

✓ He changed something about himself.

Well Trained

✓ Do not take this puzzle too seriously—it involves a bad pun.

✓ The child was correct. But why?

Razor Attack

✓ She meant to hurt him, and he did not defend himself.

✓ The razor made full contact with his unprotected throat.

✓ She could not have shaved him either.

The Old Crooner

✓ Bing Crosby himself did not take part in the action to reduce crime.

✓ His songs were used to reduce crime.

✓ His songs are old-fashioned and melodic, which means that some people like them and some do not.

Generosity?

✓ He had not intended to give any money away, and did not do so out of altruistic motives.
✓ He was under pressure.

The Parson's Pup

✓ The fact that he is religious is not relevant.
✓ The vicar is particular about his appearance.

Watch That Man!

✓ The wristwatch was perfectly legal and did not give the runner an unfair advantage.
✓ The man had cheated.
✓ The clue to his cheating was that his wristwatch had changed hands.

Quarters

✓ The quarters he needed were coins.
✓ He had discovered that his brother intended to kill him and his wife.
✓ He drove to a gas station.
✓ He had a medical condition.

Oskar

✓ Kokoschka had fought for Germany in World War I, but he was not a military man and hated war.

✓ He had applied to study art at the academy and had succeeded in gaining entry.

✓ He never met Hitler.

Drink and Die I

✓ The sign was on a restaurant.

✓ There was no evil intent.

✓ Something was not working.

Drink and Die II

✓ They did not get drunk. No vehicles were involved.

✓ They slowly drank some beer and suffocated to death.

✓ They had wanted to keep their beer very cold.

Traffic Offense

✓ He drives to work.

✓ Something had changed, but it was more fundamental than just a traffic light.

✓ How had he forgotten after all that publicity?

Bad Bump

✓ Julie and George were a woman and a man who had not met before, and they did not speak when they bumped into each other.

✓ Julie did not hurt George when she bumped into him, but shortly afterward they were both killed by a massive blow.

✓ Both were traveling, but not on any vehicle.

The Clever Detective

✓ The crime was a robbery.

✓ It took place at a border crossing.

✓ The detective saw what was missing.

The Silent Robber

✓ The security was very tight with alarms, lights, and guard dogs to deter and detect intruders.

✓ The copper that was taken was in the form of balls of wire.

✓ The copper was being systematically removed, but not by a criminal.

A Difference in Attitude

✓ He made two announcements; the first was a warning.

✓ Some passengers got off the train.

✓ The honest passengers laughed when they heard his second announcement.

Insecure

✓ The new security device was designed to deter burglars, but in some ways it helped them.

✓ The new device involved very strong lights that lit up certain areas brilliantly.

✓ The strong lights also produced something else.

Deadly Talk

✓ The President of the United States was killed as an indirect result of a speech he made.

✓ He was not assassinated. He died accidentally.

✓ The speech was his inauguration speech.

✓ It was given in Washington in March 1841.

The Fruit of Sarcasm

✓ A chef was displeased with the comments of a customer.

✓ He deliberately exaggerated certain aspects of the dish he prepared.

✓ It is now a very popular snack.

Timepiece

✓ Advertising agencies prefer a personal, positive, and friendly image. How does ten to two help this?

Racing Certainty

✓ This was a regular 100-meter race run by normal athletes competing to win.
✓ The man who ran the fastest 100 meters crossed the line second.
✓ All competitors were in the blocks at the same time and heard the starter's gun.

No Claims Bonus

✓ He did not try to defraud or cheat the insurance company.
✓ The nature of his accident is not relevant. The insurance company refused on a technical issue.
✓ The stuntman took great care to prepare for the jump. He measured the tower carefully, well in advance.
✓ Something changed about the tower.

Second of One

✓ This involves a team in a competition.
✓ They were the only contestants.
✓ They were awarded second place.

Death by Reading

✓ She read books and magazines.
✓ The topic of her reading is not relevant.
✓ She was murdered by her husband.
✓ She was poisoned.

My Condiments to the Chef

✓ There is no financial or tax advantage in producing or buying cooking wine.

✓ The benefit relates to the fact that the wine can only used for cooking.

✓ Restaurant owners prefer to use cooking wine because it reduces a risk.

Elementary

✓ This does not have to do with the weight of the boat. It is not possible to see if it is lower in the water.

✓ It does not involve the direction of the boat or anything happening on shore.

✓ This does not involve the fishing gear, the crew, or any signal from the boat.

✓ The fishermen first haul in the nets and then process the fish.

✓ They dispose of scraps they do not want.

Taking the Right Steps

✓ The men carried the ladder around the corner very easily.

✓ No mathematics or calculations are needed for the solution.

✓ Check your assumptions on this ladder.

Only in the U.S.A.

✓ The day is not named after a person, and no celebrity is involved in the day.
✓ The day does not commemorate any historical event or anything to do with the origin, politics, or history of the United States.
✓ The way the Americans write the date is relevant.
✓ Mathematicians celebrate this day.

Cheaper by the Dozen

✓ Under certain circumstances, I can reduce the bill from the energy company by using more gas.
✓ The gas is used to heat my house and water.
✓ The price of the gas per cubic foot does not become lower as more gas is used.
✓ Gas is one of the most efficient fuels for heating.

Lakeless

✓ The man was in danger but not from an animal or a person.
✓ The lake had evaporated, but the weather was not a factor.
✓ There was a natural catastrophe.

Red-Faced

✓ He knew the author.
✓ The subject of the book is not relevant. It was not undesirable in any way.
✓ The author had written a dedication in the book.

Picture Book

✓ This has nothing to do with the weather.

✓ This does not have to do with boats, but has to do with transport.

✓ The man was sending a signal.

Poor Pet

✓ A dog was sent on a journey which it did not survive.

✓ There was enormous political interest in this experiment.

High Flyer

✓ He was a passenger who caught the right plane at the right time for his destination.

✓ It was a normal flight, and the flight went smoothly.

✓ If he had been on board the plane when the engines started, then he would not have been embarrassed.

Birds of a Feather

✓ There are thought to be two main benefits to the birds. One has to do with energy.

✓ Why not fly in a long line?

Deadly Delivery

✓ The man had nothing to do with the mail or post office.

✓ The extra mail was not informing people about the manor his death.

✓ He was a good person but not especially important inhis day.

Fatal Fork

✓ The first man killed the second man.

✓ They had not known each other before this day.

✓ The killing was not accidental.

✓ Many people witnessed the event, but the man was not charged with murder or any other crime.

Groovy Movie

✓ The director was making a film about World War II.

✓ He wanted extras for the battle scenes.

✓ The movie was Saving Private Ryan.

Double Your Money

✓ He does it for security.

✓ He intends that the notes be put back together.

Malfunction

✓ The piece of machinery was high technology.

✓ The expression refers to a fault or malfunction.

A Friendly Match?

✓ They were not professional or even regular football players.

✓ They were not criminals, but they were enemies.

✓ This happened in France.

Lifesaver

✓ The newspaper did not directly protect him from a weapon or from danger.

✓ It did not staunch a wound.

✓ It was that same day's newspaper, and it served as information that helped save him.

The Plant

✓ The policeman was not trying to frame or incriminatethe woman. He was trying to find out the truth.

✓ The woman did not know the bag was there until shewas told about it.

✓ The bag looked as though it might be drugs.

✓ This was not a training exercise.

Memory Transplant

✓ The operation was not a transplant or a brain operation.

✓ He tended to forget where he put things.

✓ He still forgot things after the operation; however, it meant that he had one less thing to worry about.

The Kitty's Ming

✓ The cat and its food are not important.

✓ He is aware that the bowl is very valuable.

✓ He hopes that people will notice, but he's not trying to impress them.

✓ He does it for financial gain.

Stranger Danger

✓ The stranger was a human.

✓ They were expecting him.

✓ He did not perform a service for them.

✓ Although he did not say a word, he did utter some sounds.

The Lethal Lie

✓ Criminals who wanted to know where some money washidden interrogated the man.

✓ He answered truthfully and told where the money was.

✓ The criminals and the man were deceived.

✓ There was a language issue.

Focus Pocus

✓ For the hour, the guard pointed his head toward the gemand kept looking at it.

✓ The clever thief managed to switch the gem even whilethe guard thought he was looking at it.

✓ No visual trickery or mirrors were involved.

✓ The thief got the guard to close his eyes momentarily.

Outrage

✓ They were husband and wife.

✓ No one, not even the most sensitive, was offended.

First Time, Last Time

✓ This historical event was not a dance as such.
✓ He did not do it to entertain the audience. He did not want
  to do it.
✓ The dancer's body performed powerful and involuntarygyrations.

Speechless

✓ Pierre was punished.
✓ He saw the people momentarily.
✓ He had been held in prison.

Meeting and Greeting

✓ The woman would normally have shaken hands withher friend,
  but today she was not able to.
✓ She was rushing today, but her hurry was not the only reason that
  she did not shake hands with her friend.
✓ She was rushing to the hospital.
✓ She had suffered a serious accident.

Playacting

✓ The play that the rich man saw was well produced and well acted.
✓ The producer kept his word to the man, but not in the way that
  the man had expected.
✓ The play the man wrote appeared on the stage.

The Uneaten

✓ The boy and girl were healthy and enjoyed chocolate.

✓ The eggs were unusual.

✓ They were a royal family.

Walk of Death

✓ She was not murdered.

✓ She was killed in a freak accident.

✓ Heavy blows killed her where she was found.

✓ No one removed the items that killed her, but nothing was found.

Defensive Measure

✓ It was found that fences provided better security than walls.

✓ More burglars were caught and more were deterred.

✓ Fences have gaps.

Shaping the World

✓ The shape was personal to him.

✓ He copyrighted it to protect his personal image.

✓ He was Russian.

The Shot That Saved

✓ The photo revealed a life-threatening condition.

✓ The photograph was of the boy's face.

✓ She used flash photography.

False Confession

✓ The man had not shot anyone, and he had not committed a crime other than misleading the police.

✓ He was frustrated with the police.

✓ He wanted the police to apprehend some criminals.

Garment for Rent

✓ By destroying the sweater, he saved his life.

✓ The sweater was never a danger to him.

✓ He put the sweater to another use.

Key Decision

✓ This is not a normal building.

✓ The door can be opened with this key, but the man cannot open the door.

✓ A security feature prevents him from opening the door.

A Long Way to Go for a Drink

✓ The man was not going on vacation. There was no other reason for his trip than to visit a bar.

✓ He did not meet anyone.

✓ Any bar would do after he reached his destination.

✓ Drinking was not his only vice.

Pop the Question

✓ The woman was not wearing anything that would give an indication of her decision.

✓ The man deduced that she would refuse his offer of marriage.

✓ It was related to what she ate.

Custom and Practice

✓ Mark Twain cleverly described the drink.

✓ He justified it as an article of clothing.

✓ What could he have called it?

Towitt, Towoo

✓ Someone deliberately placed the stuffed owl in the tree.

✓ The owl was not there to advise people about hunting. It also wasn't intended to deter or warn other creatures or people.

✓ A shopkeeper put it there to aid business.

✓ The owl did not carry any signage or advertising.

Plane Puzzler

✓ All the plane's engines were turned off, and they closed down.

✓ The plane did not glide or use a balloon, parachute, or lighter-than-air gases.

✓ The plane continued to fly but not under its own power.

High Caliber

✓ The man did not wear any protective clothing.

✓ A gun was involved but no bullets.

✓ They were entertainers.

Wounded Enemy

✓ He did not act out of kindness or mercy.

✓ The men were deadly enemies in opposing armed forces.

✓ Winning the war was more important than killing every enemy.

Smoking Is Bad for You

✓ The husband acted to protect himself and his wife.

✓ The man in the broom closet was a threat to the man and woman.

✓ The wife did not normally smoke.

Determined to Die

✓ Jacques died, but not from a gunshot.

✓ He also did not die from hanging or poison.

✓ He did not die from the fire.

Hello, Grandma!

✓ The grandmother was as normal as a grandmother can be.

✓ The grandmother did not do, say, or wear anything embarrassing.

✓ The presence of the grandmother demonstrated a deceit.

Cake Killer

✓ There was nothing poisonous or unhygienic about the cake, the plate, or her hands.

✓ It was a sugary cake, and some of the sugar stayed on her hands.

✓ She had a medical condition.

Vacation, Vacation, Vacation

✓ The bank is acting out of self-interest.

✓ There are financial benefits to the bank for the two-week break, but it has nothing to do with vacation pay or employee benefits.

✓ The bank is concerned about fraud.

Clerical Advantage

✓ It is something religious.

✓ It is not a title, name, rite, or costume.

✓ It is not used while you are alive.

Bad Loser

✓ The loser used a real gun with real bullets with the intention of harming his opponent.

✓ The man and his opponent were competing against each other to win the prize.

✓ The man was playing a board game.

Puppy Love

✓ The dog did something that showed that the children were misbehaving.

✓ The children were at school.

✓ The dog did something that it had been trained to do.

✓ The dog did not belong to a teacher, and it did not belong to any of the children.

Death at the Door

✓ The woman was not under attack.

✓ She was not at home or at work.

✓ There was in no danger from fire.

✓ The door and window would normally open correctly. However, she was unable to open either of them because of the situation in which she found herself.

The Lethal Warning

✓ His warning caused the very danger he feared.

✓ He was killed in an accident.

✓ His friend heard his warning.

✓ No one else was involved.

Field of Gold

✓ The golden dye did not serve any agricultural purpose.

✓ Someone asked him to change the appearance of the field.

✓ It was for an artistic purpose.

Good Bump

✓ It was her car, and she was not trying to damage it.

✓ She was not in danger.

✓ She had forgotten something.

Timeless

✓ This woman is not a film star, actress, television personality, politician, or pop star.

Chilly

✓ A desert is defined as a place with very little or no precipitation.

The Silly Salesman

✓ The salesman was not testing a product.

✓ He did not sell dangerous products.

✓ He drove to his appointment.

✓ He died in a car accident.

It's Not True!

✓ She was an English teacher.

✓ She was teaching the value of correct punctuation.

Not Here, Son

✓ The boy wanted to practice a particular athletic event.

✓ He was a runner.

✓ People considered what he did disrespectful.

Unsanitary Janitor

✓ The janitor was following instructions.
✓ Although what he did was unhygienic, he did it with worthy motives.
✓ He worked at a school.
✓ His action was designed to improve behavior.

Hyper-Inflation

✓ It was not a particularly rare or unusual vintage of wine.
✓ The bottle became valuable as a collector's item.
✓ This involves some celebrities.

THE ANSWERS

The Deadly Sculpture

He lived in a tower on a hill. Being poor, he had no money for materials, so he took the copper lightning rod from the building. He made a beautiful statue with the copper, but soon afterward the tower was struck by lightning and he was killed.

Peak Performance

In the climber's knapsack was his national flag, which he would have planted on the summit had he reached it.

The Fatal Fish

The man's boat had capsized and he was adrift in an inflatable dinghy in a cold ocean. He caught a fish and, while cutting it up, his knife slipped and punctured the dinghy.

Adam Had None

The letter e.

Shot Dead

The woman was a Russian sniper who, during the siege of Stalingrad in World War II, shot several German soldiers.

Would You Believe It?

The second person was underwater, so the block floated up. The third person was on a space station, where there was no gravity, so when the block was released it floated unsupported.

Jailbreak

The man knew that his escape would be detected after about half an hour. He escaped at 10:30 on Tuesday morning just 30 minutes before the routine weekly alarm test, when everyone in the surrounding area would ignore the siren.

Sitting Ducks

The woman is an aeronautics engineer. She uses the gun to shoots ducks at airplane engines to test how they handle high-speed impacts with birds.

Bald Facts

After Mary, Queen of Scots had been beheaded, the executioner held up her head to show it to the mob. The head fell out of the wig.

Lethal Action

The Brazilian customs authorities require that all imported fruit be sprayed with pesticides to prevent insects or diseases from reaching domestic crops. They sprayed the hold of a fruit ship arriving from the Ivory Coast in Africa just before it docked in Brazil. They subsequently found the bodies of 10 stowaways who had hidden in the ship's hold and who had been poisoned by the pesticides.

Recognition

His Aunt Mary and his mother were identical twins.

Destruction

The body of a very overweight man is being cremated. There is so much fat that the crematorium catches fire and is burned down.

Pesky Escalator

The foreign visitor saw a sign saying, "Dogs must be carried." He did not have a dog!

Wonderful Walk

During his walk in the woods, the man picked up several burrs on his clothes. When he returned home, he examined them under his microscope and discovered the mechanism whereby they stick on. He went on to invent Velcro.

Poles Apart

Before the expedition the explorers deliberately ate a lot of fatty foods and put on several pounds of extra weight so that the fat would serve as food and fuel.

Arrested Development

The bank robber dashed to the revolving door and tried to push it in the direction in which it would not revolve.

Holed Out

The golfer's ball rebounded off the head of another golfer who was crossing the green. The ball bounced into the hole. However, the man who was hit died.

Trunk-ated

A policeman suspects that there is the body of a murdered man in the trunk. He dials the cell phone of the victim and the phone is heard ringing in the trunk.

Sports Mad

The man wanted to record his favorite football team on TV. However, the safety tab on his only videocassette had been removed and he needed to cover the space with tape.

Appendectomy I

The patient was a man who was going on a polar expedition in the first years of the 20th century. If he got appendicitis in such a remote region, he would die due to lack of treatment, so his healthy appendix was removed as a precaution.

Appendectomy II

Shell shock was not recognized as a genuine medical condition during World War I. Sympathetic surgeons often removed perfectly healthy appendixes from shell-shock victims so they could be sent home on medical grounds.

Riotous Assembly

The institution was a university. Rioting students had raided the geology department and used rock samples as ammunition.

Kneed to Know

The wife of the deaf Thomas Edison used to go with him to the theater. She drummed out on his knee in Morse code with her fingers what the actors were saying on stage.

Bad Trip

The anti-drug agency distributed pencils that had TOO COOL TO DO DRUGS printed on them. As the children sharpened the pencils down, the message became—COOL TO DO DRUGS and eventually just DO DRUGS.

Two Letters

The man is given the world's most difficult crossword and offered a prize of $100 for every letter he gets right. He puts "S" for each initial letter and "E" in every other space. S is the commonest initial letter and E the commonest letter in the English language.

Body of Evidence

The woman is a cleaner who wipes the fingerprints from a murder weapon in the course of her dusting.

Shakespeare's Blunder

The identical twins Viola and Sebastian are different sexes. This is impossible.

No Charge

The man was totally deaf, so he did not hear his rights being read to him by the arresting officer.

Pond Life

Because silk hats came into fashion, the demand for beaver hats decreased. More beavers meant more small lakes and bogs.

Shoe Shop Shuffle

One shop puts left shoes outside as samples; the other three shops put right shoes out. Display shoes are stolen, but the thieves have to form pairs, so more are taken from the store showing left shoes.

Caesar's Blunder

Since the tides in the Mediterranean are very weak, Julius Caesar did not beach his ships high enough when he landed on the shores of England. Many ships floated off on the next tide and were lost.

Slow Death

Aeschylus was killed when the tortoise was dropped on him from a height by an eagle who may have mistaken the bald head of Aeschylus for a rock on which to break the tortoise.

Driving Away

The rich woman was very nearsighted, but did not like wearing glasses or contact lenses. So she had her windshield ground to her prescription. The thief could not see clearly through it.

Lit Too Well?

During the blitz in World War II, London was subjected to heavy bombing by German planes. Sussex is south of London. It is on the flight path from Germany and part of its coastline resembles the Thames estuary. The authorities put lights in fields and in empty countryside to look like blacked-out London from the air. Some German aircrews were deceived and dropped their bombs in the wrong place.

Quick on the Draw

The man's wife had played a trick on him. She called him to watch the drawing on TV and he was unaware that he was watching a video of the previous week's draw. She had bought him a ticket for today's draw and chosen the previous week's winning numbers.

Scaled Down

The butcher had only one turkey left. The customer asked him its weight and he weighed it. The customer then asked if he had a slightly heavier one, so the butcher put the turkey away and then brought it out again. This time when he weighed it, he pressed down on the scale with his thumb in order to give it an exaggerated weight. The customer then said, "Fine—I'll take both!"

The Happy Woman

She was playing golf and hit an eagle—two under par and a very good score.

Vandal Scandal

The authorities arranged for some chips of marble from the same original quarry source as the Parthenon to be distributed around the site every day. Tourists thought that they had picked up a piece of the original columns and were satisfied.

The Deadly Drawing

She entered the room and saw the chalk picture outline of a body on the floor. It was the site of a recent murder and the chalk marked the position of the body.

Leonardo's Secret

Leonardo hid the secret designs by painting over them with beautiful oil paintings. He knew that no one would remove such masterpieces. But he did not know that modern x-ray techniques would allow art historians to see through the oil paintings and reveal his designs.

Down Periscope

The submarine started at sea and then sailed into a canal system, where each lock dropped the water level by 30 feet.

The Letter Left Out

The letter W is left out because it can always be written as UU—double U!

Arrested Development—Again

Bank employees noticed that the two men were Siamese twins. This reduced the number of suspects dramatically.

Titanic Proportions

One of the reasons why so many perished on the Titanic was the shortage of lifeboats. Laws were passed to ensure that all ships had adequate lifeboats for all crew and passengers. One small ship took on so many lifeboats that it sank under their weight. (It must have been overloaded already!)

The Mover

The letter t.

Death of a Player

The man was a golfer who absentmindedly sucked on his tee between shots. The tee had picked up deadly weed killer used on the golf course, and the man died from poisoning.

Hot Picture

The woman commissioned a tattoo artist to produce a beautiful tattoo on her husband's back as a birthday present. The picture was fine, but the next day the unfortunate man was killed in a motorcycle accident. He was cremated.

Genuine Article

The play was written by Brian Shakespeare, a contemporary dramatist. He vouched for its authenticity.

Unhealthy Lifestyle

The man was a heavy smoker. His smoke kept away mosquitoes and other insects. The woman died from an insect bite.

New World Record

The woman's great-great-granddaughter gave birth, so the old woman became the only known great-great-great-grandmother alive. The family had six generations alive at the same time.

Death by Romance

The couple spent their honeymoon on a trip to the Arctic. They stayed in an igloo. The fire melted a hole in the roof and they died of exposure.

Penalty

It was the women's World Cup and the match was played in a country with strict rules about female nudity or undressing in public.

Golf Challenge I

The woman's handicap was more than two shots greater than the man's.

Golf Challenge II

They were playing match play. The woman won more holes than the man.

Golf Challenge III

They were playing darts—highest score with three darts.

Poor Investment

The house was in a beautiful clifftop location. But within a few years, coastal erosion accelerated, and nothing could stop the house from eventually falling into the sea.

Give Us a Hand ...

The man was a diver searching for pearls in giant clams. A previous diver had had his hand trapped in the clam, and as his oxygen ran out the poor man was forced to cut off his own hand.

Evil Intent

The man happened to put his door key in his mouth (because he was holding lots of other things in his hands). The key tasted of soap. He deduced correctly that his visitor had taken an impression of the key in a bar of soap in order to make a duplicate key so that he could be burgled.

Two Heads Are Better Than One!

They were Native Americans who saw a European riding a horse. It was the first time they had seen a horse.

Stone Me!

David slew Goliath with a stone from his sling and a major battle was averted.

Judge for Yourself

The defendant sent the judge a cheap box of cigars and included the plaintiff's name card in it!

Love Letters

She was a divorce lawyer drumming up business!

Strange Behavior

The man saw a tree lying across the road. He was in Africa and he knew that blocking the road with a tree was a favorite trick of armed bandits, who then waited for a car to stop at the tree so that they could ambush and rob the passengers. He guessed correctly that this was the case here, so he reversed quickly to avoid danger.

Tree Trouble

The foundation of the wall cut through the roots of the ancient tree and killed it.

The Burial Chamber

The man was building the burial chamber of an Egyptian pharaoh in ancient times. He built the real burial chamber deep inside a pyramid. He also built another burial chamber that was easier to find that he deliberately wrecked so that when any future graverobbers found it, they would think that earlier graverobbers had found the tomb and taken the treasure.

Miscarriage of Justice

The Italian was Pontius Pilate, who released Barabbas and condemned Jesus Christ to die by crucifixion at Easter time. Every year Easter is marked by the sale of millions of chocolate Easter eggs worldwide.

Offenses Down

The police officers filled in their reports and forms while sitting in marked police cars parked outside the homes of known criminals. Drug dealers, fences, and burglars found it very inhibiting and bad for business to have a marked police car outside their houses. So crime went down.

Police Chase

The getaway vehicle was a double-decker bus that went under a low bridge. The top deck of the bus was cut off and fell onto the pursuing police car. (This is a famous scene in a movie featuring James Bond, Agent 007.)

Café Society

The café owner installed pink lighting that highlighted all the teenagers' acne!

Hi, Jean!

The shop owner introduced an electric insect zapper to kill flies and other insects that might land on the food. However, when the flies were "zapped," they were propelled up to five feet, and often fell on the food.

The Empty Machine

Kids had poured water into molds the size of quarters. The molds were placed in the deep freeze and the resulting ice coins were used in the machine. They subsequently melted and dripped out of the machine leaving no trace.

Take a Fence

The man had made green paint by mixing yellow paint and blue paint. The blue paint was oil-based, but the yellow paint was water-based. Heavy rain had dissolved the yellow paint, leaving the fence decidedly blue.

Sex Discrimination

It was found that the female lawyers wore underwire bras, which set off the very sensitive metal detectors.

Weight Loss

The doctor running the clinic had noticed that people living at high altitudes were generally thin. The air is thinner and people use more energy in all activities, including breathing. He therefore located his diet clinic at 8,000 feet above sea level and the patients found that they lost weight.

Psychic

You notice that the woman is carrying a kettle. It is a very cold morning and only one of the cars has the windshield de-iced. You deduce correctly that she has defrosted her windshield with the kettle and is returning it to her home before setting off on her journey.

The Happy Robber

The man was robbing a blood bank. He stole some rare blood that his sick daughter needed for a life-saving operation. He could not have afforded to buy the blood.

Siege Mentality

Several of the attacking soldiers had died of the plague. Their bodies were catapulted over the walls, and they infected many of the defenders, who were in a much more confined space. The defenders soon surrendered.

Carrier Bags

It was seriously proposed that the British Navy tow icebergs from the north and shape the tops to serve as aircraft carriers. They could not be sunk, lasted quite a long time, and could be cheaply replaced. However, it was too lateral a solution for the Navy high command!

The Cathedral Untouched

On a moonlit night, the dome of St. Paul's cathedral acted like a shining beacon to guide German planes during the blackout, so they deliberately avoided bombing it.

Bags Away

The passenger's pet dog escaped from his suitcase in the hold and bit through some of the plane's electric cables, thereby disrupting the plane's controls.

The Sad Samaritan

Jim found the full gas can in the trunk of his car. He had driven off and left the motorist stranded.

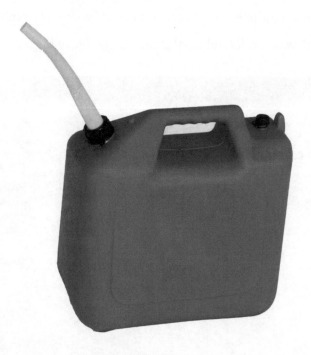

The Tallest Tree

The men chopped down the tree and then measured it on the ground!

The Unwelcome Guest

The couple gave the neighbor a good meal, and when he finished, they gave his scrap-filled plate to the dog, who proceeded to lick it clean. They then put the plate straight back into the cupboard—pretending that was their normal procedure. The neighbor did not come back for any more meals!

Poor Show

His name was Dick Fosbury, inventor of the famous Fosbury flop, a new high-jumping technique that involved going over the bar backward and that revolutionized the sport. He won the gold medal in the Mexico City Olympics in 1968.

Message Received

Alexander the Great had the envoy's head shaved and then the message was tattooed on the envoy's head. Then he let the man's hair grow for a few weeks. When the envoy arrived, his head was shaved to reveal the message.

The Mighty Stone

The peasant first suggested putting props around the boulder to stabilize it. Then a team of workers dug a big hole around and halfway under the boulder. When the hole was big enough, they pulled away the props and the boulder rolled into the hole where it was then covered with earth.

The World's Most Expensive Car

The most expensive car was the moon buggy used by astronauts to explore the moon. It was left there. Although NASA would like to sell it, no one can retrieve it!

The Fatal Fall

The woman was running in the Olympics in her national relay team. She dropped the baton and her team ended up losing. When she later returned to her country, the tyrannical despot who ran it was so displeased that he had her shot.

Election Selection

The successful candidate changed his name to "None of the Above." His name appeared on the list below the other candidates (Davies, Garcia, and Jones). The voters in the deprived area resented all the established political parties and voted for None of the Above as a protest.

Well Trained

The child was correct. It was a mail train!

Razor Attack

The woman forgot to plug in the razor!

The Old Crooner

The owners of shopping malls found that if they used Bing Crosby songs for the music in the public areas, then they had fewer undesirable youngsters hanging around and less crime was committed.

Generosity?

The man robbed a bank and was chased on foot by the public and the police. He threw away much of the cash he had acquired, which caused some chasers to stop to pick up the money and caused a rumpus that delayed the police and allowed the criminal to escape. The people who picked up the bills were forced to give them back or face prosecution.

The Parson's Pup

The vicar wears black suits and knows that light-colored dog hairs will show up on his suits, but that black ones will not be noticed.

Watch That Man!

A picture of the runner early in the race showed him wearing his watch on his right wrist. When he crossed the finishing line, it was on his left wrist. The judges investigated further and found that one man had run the first half of the race and his identical twin brother had run the second half. They had switched at a toilet on the route.

Quarters

The man has learned that his brother planned to kill him and his wife in order to take over the family business. The man was driving through the desert to warn his wife that his brother was going to kill her. He intended to kill his brother, but he was diabetic and had to stop for sugar. He reached a gas station, but it was closed and he had no change. He could not make the phone call to save his wife (one quarter). He could not get something sweet from the vending machine (two quarters). Hence he died and his brother killed his wife.

Oskar

Oskar Kokoschka (1886–1980) applied to study at the Academy of Arts in Vienna in 1907. A young man called Adolf Hitler also applied. Oskar was successful but Hitler just missed being accepted. Had Hitler taken Oskar's place, it is likely he would have followed art rather than politics as a career.

Drink and Die I

It was a restaurant that had a neon sign that said "Drink and Dine." Unfortunately, the light in the third letter N had failed.

Drink and Die II

They went caving and took some beers with them in a cooler (cool box) packed with dry ice to keep the beer cold. They opened the box. The dry ice melted and formed carbon dioxide. Because carbon dioxide is denser than air, it drove the oxygen out of the small, low cave. They suffocated to death.

Traffic Offense

The man was a Swedish motorist who drove to work on the left side of the road as he had for the previous twenty years. Unfortunately for him, it was on the day that Sweden changed over to driving on the right-hand side of the road.

Bad Bump

Julie and George were both skydivers. George had his parachute deployed when Julie crashed into it. It collapsed around her, thus preventing her from opening her parachute.

The Clever Detective

A thief had stolen two letters from the sign at the border that said "Welcome to the USA." Now it said "Welcome to the U."

The Silent Robber

The security guards had a German Shepherd, that roamed the factory. It took the bright balls of copper and buried them in the factory yard.

A Difference in Attitude

As the train pulled into the station, the driver announced over the public-address system: "There will be a team of ticket inspectors entering at the next station, so those without a valid ticket may want to leave here." Many people left the train. As the driver closed the doors and set the train in motion again, he announced through the external speakers: "I was just joking."

Insecure

The security device cast much brighter lights outside dwellings. Brighter lights cast more intense shadows, which burglars used for better hiding places.

Deadly Talk

William Henry Harrison (1773–1841) was the ninth president of the United States and the first to die in office. He gave an inaugural speech in the cold Washington drizzle in March 1841. The speech lasted 100 minutes and he did not wear a hat or coat. He contracted pneumonia and died a month later.

The Fruit of Sarcasm

In a restaurant, the chef was annoyed by a customer who kept sending back his French fries, complaining that they were too thick and not crispy enough. So the chef cut the potatoes as thinly as he possibly could, and fried them so that they were as crisp as possible. These became the potato chips we know today.

Timepiece

The idea seems to have come from Japan, and the configuration looks like a happy, smiling face.

Racing Certainty

This is supposed to have happened to Carl Lewis. Although he ran the 100 meters faster than anyone else, his starting reaction time was slow. This meant that he did not start until 0.05 seconds had elapsed. The race was won by somebody who started after 0.03 seconds, and although Lewis ran the 100 meters faster than the winner, he came in second.

No Claims Bonus

The stuntman insures himself to jump off a tower that is 300 meters tall. He measures it in winter and insures himself to jump from that height. But the jump takes place in summer when, due to expansion of the metal, the tower is several centimeters (a few inches) taller. The insurance company refuses to pay his injury claim.

Second of One

In Arklow, Ireland, in the County of Wicklow, an annual music festival is held. In the contest for choirs in 1978, there was only one entrant. The Dublin Welsh Male Voice Choir, despite being the only contender in a field of one, managed to come in second. Because they had arrived an hour late, the judges did not award them first prize.

Death by Reading

While on a business trip, a man sends his wife a magazine. Aware of her habit of licking her finger before turning each page, he puts poison on the corners of several pages. The poison transfers from page to finger to mouth, thus killing her.

My Condiments to the Chef

Wine flavored with salt and pepper is sold to hotels and restaurants for use in cooking. They do not want to buy ordinary wine because they fear that kitchen staff will drink it.

Elementary

She saw a flock of seagulls following the boat. Seagulls prefer that someone else does the fishing so that they can easily collect the scraps. Fishermen throw scraps from their haul overboard.

Taking the Right Steps

They were carrying a rope ladder.

Only in the U.S.A

On March 14th every year in the United States, some people celebrate Pi = 3.14 day, which is not a possible date on the European calendar. (In Europe, when dates are given, the day always precedes the month: 14.3.)

Cheaper by the Dozen

My energy company supplies both gas and electricity. I get one bill for both. I previously used the electric immersion heater to provide my hot water. When I turned the gas thermostat up, I used a lot more gas but no electricity for heating water. Using gas to heat water is a lot cheaper than electricity, hence the reduction in the bill.

Lakeless

A volcano had erupted nearby. When the man reached the site of the lake, the molten lava had reached the other side and caused the lake to evaporate. He knew that it would now reach him soon.

Red-Faced

George Bernard Shaw was browsing in a second-hand bookshop one day when he found a book he had signed, "With compliments, George Bernard Shaw," and given to a friend. The friend had sold it to the shop. Shaw bought the book and inscribed it, "With renewed compliments, George Bernard Shaw," and sent it again to the friend. The friend was mortified.

Picture Book

The man who drew a ship on the map of the Atlantic Ocean was a television weather forecaster who was sending a message to his wife to pick him up after work because he had no other means of transport. This happened in the early days of the Irish television weather service before cell phones.

Poor Pet

The first artificial earth satellite was launched by the Soviet Union in 1957. The cosmonaut called Laika died in the experiment because he was unable to withstand the temperature and pressure. Laika was a dog.

High Flyer

As he walked toward the aircraft, its engines started and his wig was blown off.

Birds of a Feather

It reduces air resistance on the flock, and each bird has a clear view of what's in front. As with Olympic indoor cyclists, each bird takes a turn doing the more demanding front-flying task.

Deadly Delivery

The man was a Christian martyr called Valentine, whose feastday was declared by the pope in the fifth century. Valentine's Day on February 14 celebrates his memory. Nowadays it is the signal for millions of valentine cards to be sent. According to estimates, one billion valentine cards are sent each year, second only to Christmas cards.

Fatal Fork

The man was a gladiator in ancient Rome. His weapons were a trident (a fork-shaped spear) and a net. His task was to fight another man to the death for the entertainment of the crowd.

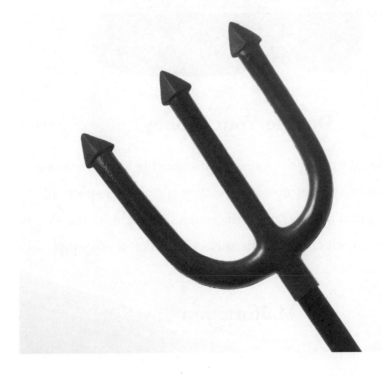

Groovy Movie

Director Steven Spielberg came to Ireland to film Saving Private Ryan. He needed extras for the D-Day landing scenes. His particular need was for people who had only one leg or one arm. They were made up to look like able-bodied soldiers, and then in the movie they had the "extra" limbs blown off to simulate what happens in battle.

Double Your Money

The man needed to send the money to his son. He knows, however, that letters are often intercepted and money is stolen. He posts all the left halves of the notes separately from all the right halves. When his son receives both envelopes, he sticks the banknotes together again.

Malfunction

He found a moth inside a prototype computer, which has led to the phrase "a computer bug."

A Friendly Match?

At Christmas in 1914 on the western front in World War I, the English and German soldiers fraternized and played a friendly game of football. Afterward, they went back to their trenches and to the war.

Lifesaver

The man was a hostage taken by kidnappers. Those who paid his ransom needed proof that he was still alive. He held a copy of the day's newspaper against his chest and was photographed to prove he was alive. Thereafter, the ransom was paid and the man was released.

The Plant

In a theater, two women were disputing the ownership of a very expensive coat. The police were called, and a policeman slipped the bag with talcum powder into a coat pocket and took it out in the presence of the two women. The impostor said, "That's not my coat!" But the real owner said, "I don't know how that got in there!"

Memory Transplant

The man kept forgetting his glasses, so he had laser eye surgery to improve his eyesight.

The Kitty's Ming

The man has an antique shop containing mostly junk, except for one very precious Ming bowl. He leaves it on the floor with some milk in it as the cat's feeding bowl. A typical dealer comes into the shop, sees all the useless rubbish, and is about to leave when he sees the precious bowl on the floor with the cat feeding from it. Reckoning that the owner is unaware of the bowl's value, he gets the bright idea of buying the cat for, say, $50, to which the owner reluctantly agrees. As he is leaving, he says, "Maybe the cat will be lonely without his little bowl. Will you throw it in for another $20?" "No," smiles the antique shop owner. "That is my lucky bowl. Why, I sell about twenty cats a week because of that little bowl!"

Stranger Danger

A baby boy was born in the house, but he lived for only a week. Naturally, his family mourned his passing away.

The Lethal Lie

The man was captured and being interrogated by the Mafia. He had stolen a huge amount of money from them and hidden it away. However, he did not speak their language, and they did not speak his, so they had to use an interpreter. Through the interpreter, they tell him that if he speaks the truth, he will not be killed. Then they tell him (all through the interpreter) that if he does not tell them where the money is, they will kill him. In fear, he tells the interpreter that the money is hidden at a certain address. The interpreter then says to the Mafia, "He won't tell you because he doesn't think you have the guts to kill him." So they take the man out and shoot him, and of course the interpreter later collects all the money.

Focus Pocus

The thief sprayed some pepper spray near the guard. The guard sneezed, and it is well known that you cannot sneeze with your eyes open. During these few seconds, the thief substituted a fake for the real jewel.

Outrage

The cartoon characters Fred and Wilma Flintstone were the first couple to appear in the same bed together on television.

First Time, Last Time

After having been convicted of murder, the dancer was being hanged. In the final moments of his hanging, the dancer's body, like many dying bodies, performed bizarre movements that novelist Henry Fielding called "the dance without music."

Speechless

Pierre was a criminal who was executed in France by guillotine. His severed head retained consciousness for a few seconds, during which time he could see his family but could not utter a sound.

Meeting and Greeting

The woman's hand had just been cut off in an accident, and she was hurrying to the hospital carrying it packed in ice in her handbag.

Playacting

The producer promised to put it on stage as part of a theatrical evening. He kept his promise by shredding the only copy of the script and using it as a snowstorm in another play.

The Uneaten

Nicholas, czar of Russia in the early 1900s, gave eggs made by Peter Fabergé as Easter presents for his children. The eggs were exquisitely made and became highly valued works of art.

Walk of Death

She was caught in a freak hailstorm and was bombarded with hailstones the size of tennis balls. The hailstones had all melted.

Defensive Measure

It was found that once an intruder had scaled a wall, he could not be seen breaking into the house or carrying out his crimes. A fence allowed people outside, whether neighbors or passers-by, to see an intruder and to raise the alarm.

Shaping the World

Mikhail Gorbachev, the former Russian leader, had a prominent birthmark on his head. When he found that a firm of vodka bottlers was using his name and face on their vodka bottles, he decided to copyright his name and the shape of his birthmark to prevent further misuse.

The Shot That Saved

The camera flash caused red-eye in the photo, but only in one eye. The other eye gave a white reflection. When the mother took the boy and the photo to a doctor, the boy was diagnosed with a cancerous tumor on the retina of one eye. This caused the white reflection. Red-eye is caused by the reflection from the capillaries in the back of a healthy eye. The boy's eye was operated on, the tumor removed, and his life was saved.

False Confession

When the man had been burgled the first time, he found the local police unresponsive. Several months later, when he saw two burglars in his garage, he called the police but was told no one was available. Exasperated, he called back and said, "Don't worry about those intruders. I shot them." Armed police arrived within minutes and arrested the burglars. The police complained, "I thought you said you shot them." He replied, "I thought you said no one was available."

Garment for Rent

The man was lost in a mine with many passages. He unraveled the sweater in order to leave a trail of thread that would allow him to trace his path out of the maze.

Key Decision

The man is trying to break into No. 10 Downing Street, the residence of the British Prime Minister. The key is fine, but for security reasons, No. 10 has a keyhole on the inside but not on the outside of the door.

A Long Way to Go for a Drink

The man wanted to smoke with his drink, and that was against the law in his country. Ireland made smoking illegal in public places in 2004. That's when many Irishmen began to travel to England in order to both smoke and drink.

Pop the Question

At their final dinner together, the woman ordered the least expensive item on the menu for each course. He deduced that if she had intended to accept his proposal of marriage, she would not have done this.

Custom and Practice

Twain said, "I use it as a nightcap!"

Towitt, Towoo

The forest was opposite a shopping center. In that shopping center was a shop that sold powerful binoculars. Customers who wanted to test the power of the binoculars could stand near the shop window and focus outside on the distant stuffed owl.

Plane Puzzler

The plane had just been picked up by another plane, a giant aircraft carrier, and so its engines could be safely switched off.

High Caliber

They were circus performers. The man was shot out of a cannon and landed in a net. One day, when he was ill, his wife took his place. Because she was lighter, she flew farther through the air, missed the net, and was killed on impact with the floor.

Wounded Enemy

This is classic military strategy. If you kill a soldier of the enemy, you reduce their forces by one. He just lies there, and the enemy may or may not bury him. But if you injure the enemy soldier so severely that he cannot fight again, he becomes a huge drain on the enemy's resources—men to rescue him and carry him off the battlefield, medical supplies, doctors, nurses, hospital supplies, rehabilitation, compensation, transport, psychological support, pension, etc.

Smoking Is Bad for You

The husband and wife had been threatened by a gangster. The couple had agreed to a code to signal danger. If the husband ever returned home and found his wife smoking a cigarette, he would know that danger was immediate. Furthermore, they agreed that she would point the cigarette in the direction of the danger. That way the husband knew that the gangster was hiding in the broom closet.

Determined to Die

The shot missed him but severed the rope. Jacques plunged into the sea, which put out the fire. He swallowed seawater, which made him vomit the poison. When he was washed up on shore, he was rescued but soon died of hypothermia. This reportedly happened on the coast of France, but it is probably an urban legend.

Hello, Grandma!

The office worker had taken off the previous day from work because, she claimed, she wanted to attend her only remaining grandmother's funeral.

Cake Killer

The woman was a diabetic. She checked her blood sugar level every day by pricking her finger to produce a little drop of blood, which she checked with a glucometer. However, since she had eaten a sugary cake with her fingers and had not washed her hands, quite an amount of sugar remained on her fingers. That sugar contaminated the tiny sample and gave a reading of sugar in her bloodstream way above what it actually was. The usual treatment for a high sugar reading is an immediate injection of insulin to use up the sugar (which, however, wasn't there!). This killed her.

Vacation, Vacation, Vacation

The bank analyzes trading patterns for any irregularities that might indicate fraud. If an employee, or trader, is absent for two weeks, that's enough time to allow the bank to discover any abnormal trading patterns he may have been involved in.

Clerical Advantage

According to medieval church custom, a bishop could have seven crosses on his tomb or gravestone, priests have five, and an ordinary person just one.

Bad Loser

The man was playing in a chess competition. After losing a game of chess to a computer, the man shot his opponent.

Puppy Love

In an exercise to build goodwill, a policeman brought a police dog into a local secondary school. The children were delighted to pet the dog. However, the dog had been trained to detect drugs, and it correctly identified six children who were carrying marijuana.

Death at the Door

When driving, the woman fell asleep at the wheel of her car and plunged into a canal. Inside the car at the bottom of the canal, she called 911. The emergency operator advised her to roll down the window and swim to safety, but water had ruined the electrical motor that operated the window, so it would not open. She tried to open the door but could not because the pressure of the water was too great. Eventually, the water flowed into the car and she drowned.

The Lethal Warning

The men were skiing. When one man called out to warn his friend about the risks of an avalanche, his loud shout caused the very thing he feared.

Field of Gold

A farmer sprayed his field with golden dye because it was featured in a film about the life of Vincent van Gogh. One of van Gogh's famous paintings features a golden wheat field.

Good Bump

She had forgotten to close the trunk. As she bumped violently over the speed bump the trunk lid clicked closed.

Timeless

The Virgin Mary has appeared more often on Time magazine than any other woman.

Chilly

The coldest desert on earth is in Antarctica. The whole continent is a desert because there is virtually no precipitation there.

The Silly Salesman

As he drove along the Florida freeway at 80 mph (about 130 kph) to reach his appointment, the salesman read his sales manual. Not surprisingly, he crashed the car and was killed.

This event won a Darwin Award (for stupidity).

It's Not True!

It was an English class. The teacher showed how punctuation can change the meaning of the sentence. First she wrote, "Woman without her man is helpless." Then she wrote, "Woman! Without her, man is helpless."

Not Here, Son

The schoolboy was an avid hurdler. The only hurdles he could find were gravestones in the church cemetery. So he practiced there. The police stopped him from this irreverent behavior.

Unsanitary Janitor

At a school for teenage girls, there had been a problem. The girls applied lipstick and then kissed the mirror on the bathroom wall to check to see if their lipstick was applied evenly. The headmistress called in all the girls and showed them how the caretaker cleaned the mirror. He deliberately dipped his mop in the toilet first. From then on, none of the girls kissed the mirror.

Hyper-Inflation

The bottle was signed by all four members of the Beatles and immediately became valuable as a collector's item the night John Lennon died.

Wally Test Answers

Test I

1. Because it has more geese in it!
2. Because they all have telephone lines!
3. So that he can fit in the small spaceship.
4. Exactly where you left him!
5. One. It takes many bricks to build the house but only one brick to complete it.
6. Take away his credit cards!
7. Edam is "made" backward.
8. A mailman.
9. Wet.
10. Take away their chairs.

Test II

1. Lemon-aid
2. A lid.
3. The lion.
4. His horse was called "yet."
5. Get someone else to break the shell.
6. Because he was dead.
7. They use rope.
8. If they lifted up that leg, they would fall over.
9. Wintertime.
10. It wooden go!

Test III

1. Young men.
2. KEY. It completes the word donkey, and a key starts a car.
3. The other half.
4. As fur as you can.
5. Just above the Pair O'Shins.
6. Dwight D. Eiffel Tower.
7. It quacks up.
8. Whenever he goes to work he gets the sack!
9. The ultrasound department.

Test IV

1. He does it during the daytime.
2. If you don't know where you are going, why are you standing in line?
3. V, W, X, Y, and Z.
4. Consider the facts: One hundred rats would kill a cat.
5. Water.
6. It is a mail bag.
7. Wet rocks.
8. October is the longest month. It has 31 days, and it gains an extra hour when the clocks are turned back.
9. In the center of the ship where the funnel be.

About the Authors

Paul Sloane lives in Camberley, Surrey, England. He has been an avid collector and composer of lateral thinking puzzles for many years. He runs the Lateral Puzzles Forum on the Internet, where readers are able to pose and solve puzzles interactively: www.lateralpuzzles.com.

Sloane has his own business helping organizations use lateral thinking to find creative solutions and improve innovation. The Web site is: www.destination-innovation.com.

He is a renowned speaker and course leader. He is married with three daughters, and in his spare time he plays golf, chess, tennis, and keyboards in an aging rock band, the Fat Cats.

Des MacHale was born in County Mayo, Ireland. He lives in Cork with his wife, Anne, and their five children. He's an associate professor of mathematics at University College Cork. He has a passionate interest in puzzles of all sorts and has written over 60 books on various subjects—lateral thinking puzzles, jokes, a biography of the mathematician George Boole, insights on John Ford's film The Quiet Man, and a nine-volume Wit series of humorous quotations. He has published puzzles in the Brainteaser section of The Sunday Times of London.

MacHale's other interests include bird-watching (ah, so relaxing), classical music and Irish traditional music, book collecting, photography, old movies, tennis, quizzes, words, humor, broadcasting, and health education. In fact, he's interested in everything except wine, jazz, and Demi Moore. (Our apologies to Ms. Moore.)